AGE OF CONFIDENCE

THE NEW JEWISH CULTURE WAVE

EDITED BY DAVID BENMAYER & REBECCA TAYLOR
WITH A FOREWORD BY HOWARD JACOBSON

ELEBRATING TWENTY YEARS OF JEWISH RENAISSANCE

The
History
Press

This book has been made possible by the generous support
of Dangoor Education.

First published 2021

The History Press
97 St George's Place, Cheltenham,
Gloucestershire, GL50 3QB
www.thehistorypress.co.uk

British Library Cataloguing in Publication Data.
A catalogue record for this book is available from the British Library.

ISBN 978 0 7509 9793 5

Typesetting and origination by The History Press
Printed in the UK by T.J. Books Ltd

CONTENTS

FOREWORD

HOWARD JACOBSON

Though it is over twenty years ago, it seems only the other day that Janet Levin accosted me at a party to engage my interest in her new magazine of Jewish life and culture. She was 58, had enjoyed a successful career running her own research consultancy, and now wanted to employ her formidable energies elsewhere. I recall the phrase 'Jewish identity' passing between us. 'Oh yes,' I remember thinking, '*that*.' I wished her well, fatalistically, like one waving good-bye to a person proposing to swim solo to Australia. I never expected to hear mention of the project again.

Her ambition as I understood it – to produce a quarterly, non-academic, non-provincial magazine of Jewish art, literature and thought, that would be at once newsy and scholarly, that would review current books and exhibitions but also reawaken interest in writers and painters and thinkers of the past, that would be accessible without being trashy, that would be internationally curious without being self-apologetic, and that didn't think the only Jewish subjects Jews were interested in were the Holocaust, antisemitism, Israel, and what to wear for their sons' barmitzvahs – was admirable, bold and bound to fail. What would make it fail, in my view, was precisely the thing Janet Levin was deter-mined to eschew: parochialism.

Sometime in the 1980s, while living in London and going through a bad marital patch, Philip Roth famously wiped his hands of British Jews. We were uninteresting and undistinguished, he said. Too subtle for you by half, was my response. We had our reasons for keeping our heads down: we'd been in this country several centuries before, and that hadn't worked out too well; and we had found ourselves in a society, this time, that had no need or relish for that immigrant exuberance that gave America its identity. As a consequence, while American Jews sang and danced, we were learning to negotiate our rights and temper our personalities in ways that made us wise.

But there was still something in the criticism of us as frightened, philistine and incurious. Those British Jews who didn't flee to the provinces to practise dentistry and accountancy took provincialism to be rooted in Jewishness itself and turned their backs on both. Anyone passing through could be forgiven for thinking we were uncultured, when the truth of it was that we wholeheartedly embraced any culture that wasn't our own. Quite simply, those wanting to avoid embarrassment, or hoping to find stimulus outside their daughters' batmitzvahs, looked beyond anything they believed Jewishness could provide. Hence the fatalistic smile with which I greeted Janet Levin's hopes for a magazine optimistically to be called *Jewish Renaissance*.

But she, and her subsequent editor Rebecca Taylor, proved me wrong. In the pages of *Jewish Renaissance* British Jewry shows as vibrant, cultivated, critical, artistically magnanimous, quick and funny and completely open to the winds of exultation or anxiety blowing in from elsewhere. It has turned out to be anything but insular and parochial. That this represents a change in English Jewish society from the one visiting American Jews sampled without joy, humour or generosity, I don't have the slightest doubt. We are no longer apologetic. We are no longer ashamed. In whatever sphere, we are confident and productive. There are many reasons for this transformation, but it is no coincidence that *Jewish Renaissance* should be around to take advantage of it. These things are symbiotic. If *Jewish Renaissance* is well positioned to record a new vitality, it is because *Jewish Renaissance* has played no small part in bringing it about.

AGE OF CONFIDENCE:
THE NEW JEWISH CULTURE WAVE

DAVID BENMAYER AND REBECCA TAYLOR

In October 2001, Janet Levin published the first issue of *Jewish Renaissance* (*JR*), a new quarterly magazine that she had been conceiving for several years. In her opening editorial, Janet explained her choice in title as well as *JR*'s purpose. She sensed a 'new desire to see Jewish culture take a confident place' in our society and the need for a publication dedicated to that objective. New initiatives were springing up elsewhere too, from the Festival of Jewish Arts and Culture in the UK to the establishment of the European Association for Jewish Culture on the continent. *JR*'s brief was to explore the array of activities on offer; to engage, challenge and excite its readers; and to raise awareness of Jewish culture, both historical and contemporary.

But there was another motivating factor for founding *JR*. Janet pointed to evidence of a parallel 'renaissance' in antisemitism and argued persuasively that our response should not be maintaining a low profile but communicating 'our heritage and traditions' to as diverse an audience as possible. This was brought more acutely into focus just days before the first issue went to press when news of the terror attacks of 11 September burst into the headlines. Janet asserted that the events of that day would change the world in immeasurable ways and that 'suddenly the launch of a new magazine … seemed an insignificant blip'. Janet persevered and reinforced *JR*'s manifesto with bold statements of intent: to 'give space to a range of views', to avoid 'inter-denominational disputes' and to 'make a positive contribution, however small, to greater understanding and tolerance in the world'. Distinguished names from across the UK Jewish community's cultural organisations joined as members of *JR*'s advisory board, but privately, many friends told Janet that her dream would not last beyond the second issue.

Changing reader preferences and a shift online were already impacting other publications. Surely, a periodical catering to a 'niche within a niche' could not buck these trends?

Eighty issues later, *JR* continues to thrive. Circulation and readership have grown continuously, and *JR*, now the UK's only publication dedicated to Jewish culture, has subscribers on every continent save for Antarctica. The magazine's features (including the 'Passport' section, which explores global Jewish communities, 'Sephardi Renaissance' and 'What's Happening') are destinations for discovering the latest events and shedding light on communities and traditions that had previously been side-lined. And in its latest development, the '*JR* Long Read', the magazine now includes an occasional series of longer pieces, the first of which was a previously unpublished story in English by Nobel Laureate Isaac Bashevis Singer.

Renaissance Publishing, *JR*'s publishing entity, has also continued to grow and professionalise. It is now a registered charity with a team of employed professionals, and *JR*'s output extends beyond the pages of the magazine alone. The 'Passport' features have been brought to life with a series of tours encountering Jewish life in Ethiopia, Uzbekistan, Myanmar and many other destinations besides. An Emerging Journalist Prize seeks to discover and nurture a future generation of writers who cover Jewish themes. Events and collaborations with partner organisations have placed *JR* on an ever-growing map of Jewish cultural organisations, events and venues. And of course, the ubiquity of the internet and social media has allowed *JR* to reach a far broader and more global audience through blogs, online articles, podcasts and streamed events – most notably during the Covid-19 pandemic and the launch of *JR*'s 'Home Entertainment' series, a regular guide to the best online arts activities.

Marking the twentieth anniversary of *JR* provides the opportunity to reflect on what, if anything, has changed since the first issue. How has the 'renaissance' of Jewish culture manifested itself? What themes have been addressed, and what impact have they had? And what can we expect of Jewish culture over the next twenty years and beyond?

To celebrate this milestone, we have invited five experts to share their assessment of the past two decades and to tackle some of the questions posed above. Covering music, art, literature, theatre and film, each of our authors has taken a differing approach, providing a distinct voice on their chosen subject. Some of the essays focus primarily on culture emanating from the UK, while others look further afield, drawing on developments in the Americas, North Africa, the Balkans and the Middle East. This was intentional. Just as with the magazine, we sought for this anthology to share a variety of views and opinions. We hope that the essays are accessible, entertaining and of interest to the lay reader as much as the specialist.

We have also interspersed each of the five sections with a selection of articles from *JR*'s archive. Selecting the material to include was tough and we are hugely grateful to Janet for her assistance with this near-impossible task. In fact, some of our favourite pieces could not be included, either because of space limitations or because they lacked relevance to the topics covered in this book. But we hope the ones that are here provide long-time readers with fond memories and those less familiar with *JR*, a taste of what the magazine offers each quarter. All the articles included can be accessed by subscribers through *JR*'s digital archive, which spans its entire twenty-year history.

One theme that emerged from all the essays commissioned for this book is the notion of confidence. In theatre, film and literature, new and established voices are exploring subjects previously considered taboo: from the challenges faced by gay Orthodox Jews to intermarriage and an examination of the tensions inherent in being Jewish and British. Jewish music, meanwhile, has been at the forefront of connecting with other cultures for at least a millennium, but in the polarised environment of a post-9/11 world, it is Sephardi and Mizrahi Jewish music, with its roots across North Africa and the Middle East, that has become a 'cultural bridge' for a greater understanding of Muslim culture in Western society. Finally, in art, the past two decades have seen a wave of predominantly female artists embarking on an 'emotional archaeology' through their work – a preoccupation with memory, where Holocaust trauma has both overshadowed and stimulated their output.

And perhaps herein lies an overarching thesis to this anthology. The past two decades began with a seismic event that shifted sentiments and made both nations and individuals question their place in this world. And yet, despite such a monumental knock in global confidence, this period has been dominated with questions of identity – an introspection that has often looked outward too. While there has certainly been a marked increase in populism, nationalism and the politics of 'us' versus 'them' in recent years (in part, a reaction to globalisation and multiculturalism), this has coincided, especially in the cultural sphere, with a new sense of confidence and 'place' for those from minority backgrounds.

And this journey can be seen in the pages of *JR*. The evolution of the magazine and the organisation reflect a growing confidence to explore all facets of Jewish identity, which often includes asking difficult questions. Indeed, *JR*'s editorial team ask themselves a series of questions when embarking on every issue: what constitutes Jewish culture? Is a subject necessarily interesting because it was created by a Jew? What is the subject's wider significance beyond the Jewish world? Sometimes the Jewish content of the work being explored is obvious – elsewhere it might be the subtext in a piece of literature or artwork that needs teasing out. The challenge for them is to ensure that the magazine lives up to its objectives of being open, critical and, above all, a place to highlight the rich diversity of the Jewish experience.

Tracing *JR*'s history can also shed some light on the history of Jewish culture writ large over the past twenty years. In the early days of *JR*, the magazine emphasised the celebration of Jewish culture, communities and thought – all still prominent today – but perhaps presented in a way to avoid ruffling too many feathers. There is a feeling of cautiousness in the early issues; of a new publication finding its feet.

But with maturity and longevity has come self-confidence. For example, *JR* was one of the first cultural organisations to put a spotlight on Sephardi culture (in large part due to the influence, imagination and immense generosity of Sir Naim Dangoor and, latterly, his son David Dangoor). Moreover, in recent years, *JR* has repeatedly addressed arts and events that challenge Jews and non-Jews and expressed views on everything from LGTBQ+ issues and Black Lives Matter to Extinction Rebellion and political developments across the world.

Of course, the confidence journey of Jewish culture did not begin twenty years ago. In researching archive material for this book, a series of three essays by Maureen Kendler were particularly instructive. Originally commissioned for *JR* in 2007, and republished after Kendler's death in 2018, the essays survey four decades of British-Jewish writing. Kendler notes that starting in the 1950s there was an 'emerging confidence' with the likes of Harold Pinter and Arnold Wesker, but that, overwhelmingly, Jewish writing in this decade 'showed a tense, uneasy community, raising its head above the parapet with confused diffidence'. The next three decades would usher forth writing that offered 'a more aggressive and thorough scrutiny of Jewish life', but the community 'would still be largely squirming, uncertain whether … all this attention was good for the Jews'.

Perhaps then, the past twenty years of Jewish culture can be summarised as representing a growing confidence coupled with a firm sense of belonging – a 'coming of age' also mirrored in the pages of *JR*. From the beginning, *JR* has emphasised the importance of being part of an international diaspora community, and increasingly, these wider influences are being reflected in mainstream British and American culture too – just think of the explosion of interest in Israeli and Middle Eastern food as popularised by Yotam Ottolenghi after opening his first UK restaurant in 2002 and the runaway success of his subsequent books. There is no doubt that the richness and diversity of Jewish culture in 2021 (particularly apparent with streamed events during the Covid-19 pandemic), not to mention its visibility on the radars of Jews and non-Jews alike, is in a far better place than it was in 2001.

And while study after study has shown that Jews across the world (apart from ultra-Orthodox communities) are choosing to move away from affiliation to a particular religious subset, this does not mean that Jews are not self-defining as Jewish. Young Jews, in particular, are increasingly likely to cite cultural identity as being more important than their religious beliefs and practices. A 2011 survey of Jewish students conducted by the Institute for Jewish Policy Research (JPR) found a much broader consensus amongst respondents on notions of their Jewish identity relating to ethnicity and culture, than they did religious practice.

And yet, the challenges will no doubt continue. As some of the essays in this collection intimate, the events of recent months and years show a worrying trend towards isolationism and mistrust that could result in the regression of culture (including Jewish culture) to a less confident place. In Jewish literature, it can already be argued that the productivity, optimism and self-confidence of mostly younger writers, have already started to dissipate in recent years.

Just as Janet could not predict how the events of 9/11 would shape the world back in 2001, it is difficult to predict how recent events may alter the landscape of Jewish culture over the next twenty years. David Baddiel's recent passionate polemic, *Jews Don't Count* (2021), is a reminder that despite the ease Jews appear to feel with their place in society, there are also reasons to be alarmed that the community is yet again facing misunderstanding and misrepresentation, particularly in contemporary culture. With *JR* and others continuing to highlight the diversity of the Jewish experience, our hope is that the voices celebrating inclusivity, awareness and diversity will continue to grow in strength.

It only remains for us to thank the people who have supported this book and, more importantly, have allowed *JR* to thrive over the past two decades and to continue its vital role today. First and foremost, Janet Levin and David Dangoor, *JR*'s founder and president respectively, for their vision and continued encouragement of all things *JR*. Ian Lancaster, *JR*'s chairman, together with all trustees past and present. *JR*'s chief executive, Aviva Dautch, and all the members of *JR*'s professional team. *JR*'s tireless volunteers on the editorial committee, as well as a back catalogue of contributors that would be too long to publish. And most of all, *JR*'s readers and supporters, without whom Janet's dream would never have been possible. Lastly, we would like to thank Nicola Guy and Juanita Hall at The History Press for their enthusiasm and dedication to this project and Sophie Hartley for her help researching images for this book.

BRITISH JEWISH LITERATURE IN THE TWENTY-FIRST CENTURY

BRYAN CHEYETTE

In his memoir, *Jacob's Gift* (2005), the journalist Jonathan Freedland writes that after 9/11, 'the question became insistent: in the great clash of civilizations, whose side are you on?' In our new century, the global repercussions of 9/11 have inevitably influenced literature because it has made the world more conflicted and Jews in Israel and the diaspora feel more vulnerable. In such a polarised world, Freedland writes, 'Jews were divided against each other but, above all, they were divided against themselves – heart against conscience, both wrestling for the soul'. If imaginative writers have anything in common, and virtually all would claim a unique vision and a personal story, it is that they thrive on internal division.

In this essay, I will be examining how writers dealt with these new socio-political challenges and I will also explore the continuities and discontinuities between twenty-first-century British-Jewish literature and its earlier incarnations. In 2003, the *Jewish Chronicle* produced a *Granta*-style list of young (those aged under 40) Jewish writers who represented a new generation of British-Jewish literature. They included Naomi Alderman, Jeremy Gavron, Zoë Heller, Charlotte Mendelson, Francesca Segal, William Sutcliffe and Adam Thirlwell, and could have included Jake Wallis Simons, Natasha Solomons and Tamar Yellin. What were the differences and similarities within this new generation and earlier generations?

Writing about contemporary literature can never be definitive as tastes in literature change, given the vast number of books published almost daily. Who to include and exclude in a literary canon is, at best, an educated guess and is guided by arbitrary validation such as literary prizes. There are connections between old and new versions of British-Jewish literature, and this will be one way of making sense of the contemporary moment. But there are also disconnections and new contexts to be considered. I have utilised the *JR* archive, among other sources, as a guide to the literary preoccupations and cultural concerns of the past two decades. This is a good match as *JR* was published one month after 9/11, which was acknowledged in its first editorial: 'Shortly before our press date the awful events happened in the US that will mean that the world will change in ways that we cannot yet comprehend.'

The editorial was prescient in anticipating a changed, newly traumatised world after 9/11 that, sadly, continues to characterise our contemporary era. At the start of the new century, *JR* indicated that global events would soon eclipse the concerns of a Jewish magazine. But the hope that it would make a 'positive contribution' to society takes the magazine back to a different era when the 'Jewish contribution to civilization' was one of the main ways in which Jews could show the world that they were good citizens. One part of the editorial looks to the future; the other part evokes the past. Such is the Janus-faced character of Jewish culture.

There were certainly reasons to be optimistic in that first editorial, even when it was written under the shadow of the burning twin towers. After all, most of the 1990s can be rightly thought of as a peak of Jewish cultural life in the diaspora, buoyed by the possibility of peace in the Middle East, which was manifested in the expansion and development of many Jewish arts organisations. The new magazine itself was a symptom of these 'boom' years and reflected these happier times in many of their articles. The *JR* continued to affirm the evolution of Jewish Studies courses, departments, and institutes in British universities; it covered the frequent exhibitions at Ben Uri (the London gallery specialising in immigrant, but particularly Jewish, art); the plethora of Jewish film, music and book festivals; and the popularity of adult education events such as Limmud, which featured speakers and seminars on all aspects of Jewish history and culture. Limmud proved so successful that permanent adult education and cultural institutions were built, such as the Jewish cultural centre, JW3, which opened on London's Finchley Road in 2013 after a ten-year gestation, or expanded, in the case of the Jewish museums in Manchester and London.

The energy and dynamism of this growth continues to be expressed in the magazine. One article rightly characterised the 1990s as the decade when closeted Jews 'came out', and this was certainly my experience. Conferences on Jewish culture and modernity were standing-room only when I expected them to be the size of a London taxi. A new kind of Jewish cultural studies came into being led by such figures as Sander Gilman, Griselda Pollock and the Boyarin brothers (the academic equivalent to the Coen brothers). One could start off researching a new topic and, five years later, be swamped by articles, doctorates and new books on the same subject. This was because a new generation of academics specialising in British-Jewish studies – David Cesarani, Tony Kushner, Sue Vice, among many others – all supervised handfuls of doctoral students. It was a good time to be alive and interested in Jewish literature and history and the arts in general. British-Jewish literature was also undergoing a revival with a variety of new voices – Linda Grant, Howard Jacobson, Elena Lappin, Simon Louvish, Clive Sinclair, William Sutcliffe, Michelene Wandor, Jonathan Wilson – joining more established voices such as Anita Brookner, Jenny Diski, Ruth Fainlight, Eva Figes, Elaine Feinstein, Gabriel Josipovici, Bernard Kops, Harold Pinter, Frederic Raphael, Bernice Rubens, Muriel Spark and Arnold Wesker.

Perhaps it was not a coincidence that the 1990s were also the boom years for Holocaust Studies, with the opening of the Washington DC Holocaust museum in 1993 and the release of Steven Spielberg's *Schindler's List* in the same year. After the fall of the Berlin Wall in 1989, access to crucial East European archives was granted for the first time, creating a parallel 'boom' in historical accounts of mass killings, in ravines and trenches, on the eastern front. One response to this new kind of history, which mapped the destruction of Jewish communities in the Soviet Union in more detail than ever before, was the growth of Jewish genealogy – and heritage in general – which also peaked in the 1990s and continues to this day. The Jewish memoir, often written by novelists and historians who were second-generation victims of the Holocaust, was rightly said to be challenging the status of literary fiction by Jews in Britain. Exemplary post-Holocaust memoirs published in the 1990s were written by Louise Kehoe, Anne Karpf and Lisa Appignanesi and continue to this day in memoirs by Jenny Diski, Elaine Feinstein, Michael Rosen and Phillipe Sands. It is in the context of cultural optimism and traumatic threat that I will explore the earlier generations of British-Jewish authors and discuss how they relate, or not, to the new generation of twenty-first-century Jewish writers in Britain.

THE SPECTRUM OF BRITISH-JEWISH LITERATURE (1945–2000)

In a 2006 lecture to mark the 350th anniversary of the readmission of Jews to England in 1656 (after their banishment by Edward I in 1290), Howard Jacobson appealed for a more confident and assertive account of Jewish life in Britain.

Rather than wallowing in the comforts of Britishness, or apologising for being 'introverted', or imitating American or Yiddish literature, Jacobson wanted to see Jews engage more robustly with the Jewish history and culture of England (and presumably also Scotland, Northern Ireland and Wales). He wanted, ultimately, to be part of a trend that reshaped 'what is meant by Englishness'. He continued:

> We have been in this country a while now. The story of our finely tuned accommodations to English culture is a fascinating one, sometimes tragic, often heroic, always funny, and never less than urgent beneath a quiescent surface. It is time we told it. We should be more interested in ourselves as English Jews.

This manifesto – on the side of localism rather than diasporism – was echoed by others who were reacting to the 1980s and 1990s. This was a time when many Jewish writers, such as Harold Pinter and Anita Brookner, chose to disguise their Jewishness, and others, such as Feinstein and Sinclair, chose to write in a diasporic mode, setting their fiction on the European continent or in the Middle East or the United States. Sinclair was quite brazen about his transcendence of Englishness and pointedly attempted to 'write fiction that owes nothing to any English antecedents'. Jacobson, in contrast, prefers to be known as the 'Jewish Jane Austen' rather than the 'English Philip Roth'.

But none of this is simple. Brookner and Pinter did, in fact, write explicitly British-Jewish literature such as Brookner's *The Latecomers* (1988) and *A Family Romance* (1993). Pinter's *Ashes to Ashes* (1996) and his early work – especially *The Birthday Party* (1958) and *The Homecoming* (1965) – have often been read as British-Jewish plays. Conversely, much of Feinstein's poetry and some of her fiction, such as *The Survivors* (1982), engaged with British-Jewish history and culture, as did Sinclair's story 'The Wingate Football Club' (1979) and his novels *Blood Libels* (1985) and *Cosmetic Effects* (1989). Most British-Jewish writers, in other words, move in and out of Britishness and Jewishness, which is an unstable spectrum rather than an easily digestible binary. A key example in our present time is Mike Leigh, who sublimates his Jewishness in all of his extraordinary plays and films since the 1970s only, in *Two Thousand Years* (2005), to write his one 'Jewish play', as he calls it.

Some insist on maintaining the binary between 'the Jew' and 'the Englishman', such as Anthony Blond, in his memoir *Jew Made in England* (2004), or John Gross's suitably euphemistic *A Double Thread: A Childhood in Mile End and Beyond* (2002). These books follow Maurice Samuel's formulaic *The Gentleman and the Jew* (1952), about growing up as an immigrant son in early twentieth-century Manchester: 'Among us Jews, as I remember vividly, the attitude toward

England was one of intense admiration, respect, gratitude, and affection.' Leigh is less patriotic (or Victorian) than his fellow Mancunian but no less binary in his outlook: 'Those of us who escaped from our Jewish background have usually spent most of our adult life keeping quiet about our Jewishness, at least in public.' I prefer to talk about a more expansive and multicultural Britishness rather than a narrow, assimilatory Englishness which is characterised by an either/or division. A spectrum of British-Jewishness is the best way to indicate this complexity. Leigh's character Tammy sums it up nicely: 'It's not the whole of me – I feel Jewish, and I don't feel Jewish.'

To illustrate this spectrum (from sameness to difference or Englishness to Jewishness) all we need to do is refer to some of the most representative Jewish writers in Britain. These go back to Grace Aguilar (1816–47), who, in her *History of the Jews of England* (1847), argued that English Jews were no different to their neighbours while, at the same time, calling for Jews to return to their Hebraic biblical roots. Israel Zangwill (1864–1926) championed, simultaneously, the ghetto and the melting pot or ethnic enclaves and ethnic transformation.

Such ambivalence can also be seen in Louis Golding, who was both an 'apt interpreter of British Jewry' in his fiction, according to *The Times*, and, also, an active campaigner for Jewish intermarriage. In her twenty-seven novels, the Booker Prize-winning Bernice Rubens (1923–2004), who was interviewed in *JR* at the end of her life, moved in and out of Jewishness, Welshness, Britishness and Europeanness. Jacobson himself could be both the poet of Jewish Manchester, and also decontextualise or dejudaise many of his other impressive fictions. And, finally, Naomi Alderman, who looks most likely to be the representative Jewish writer in our present age, has moved from transgressive stories of Orthodox Judaism in Hendon to placeless dystopias in her later work.

Jacobson's call for the experience and history of English Jews to be taken more seriously characterises some of his best novels, such as *The Mighty Walzer* (1999) and *Shylock is My Name* (2016). But it is not new. After all, Aguilar had written her history of Anglo-Jewry nearly two centuries ago and Zangwill's *Children of the Ghetto* (1892) and Golding's *Magnolia Street* (1932) could not have been more interested in 'English Jews'. Willy Goldman's important anthology, *In England and in English: A Collection of Modern Stories by Jewish Writers* (1947), shows how commonplace linking Englishness and Jewishness was just after the Second World War. According to Goldman's introduction, the anthology deals in part with 'Jewish life in England' but also contributes to a 'general British and European tradition'. Many of the most important inter-war British-Jewish writers are included in the collection, including Marghanita Laski, Ralph Finn, Henry Cohen (aka Roland Camberton), Ashley Smith and Betty Miller.

Published at a time when there were riots in English cities in response to the hanging of two British sergeants in Palestine by the Irgun (the extreme Zionist paramilitary organisation that operated in Palestine between 1931 and 1948), Goldman unsurprisingly claims that the 'material selected has no shared racial, religious or national bias'. In such circumstances it was not unusual for Goldman, a 'proletarian writer', to refuse any kind of collective Jewish identity.

Within sixteen years, British-Jewish literature virtually disappeared from equivalent collections. Gerda Charles's *Modern Jewish Stories* (1963) only included herself, Alexander Baron, Brian Glanville and Arnold Wesker out of fifteen stories. The rest were made up of Israelis (Yehuda Yaari and S. Yizhar), six North Americans (including Philip Roth, Bernard Malamud, Isaac Rosenfeld and Isaac Bashevis Singer), two South Africans (Nadine Gordimer and Dan Jacobson) and one Russian, Isaac Babel. In her introduction, Charles maintains that, after the war, the expansion of Jewish literature has been a 'great, splendid achievement' especially with 'English-speaking countries: England, the Commonwealth and, above all, America'. These 'magnificently gifted' Jewish writers were essentially global: 'In this country only a few of our writers dabbled about on the fringes.'

After such self-disparagement it is no wonder that Jacobson has called for English Jews to be 'more interested in ourselves'. Charles, a double prize-winning author, had an astonishingly short literary output which is reflected in such belittlement. Glanville's contribution to the collection marked the end of his imaginative involvement with Jewishness, following the publication of the novel *Diamond* (1962), which met with fierce criticism from the Jewish community. Wesker is a dramatist rather than a fictionist. It is ironic that, at the time, both Charles, Glanville and Wesker were hailed as initiating a 'new wave' of post-war Jewish writing in Britain. Glanville, who is in his ninetieth year, has spent the past six decades as a full-time sports journalist who publishes fiction primarily about Italy. Only his son, Mark Glanville, articulates his and his father's Jewishness in *The Goldberg Variations: From Football Hooligan to Opera Singer* (2004).

It is as if British-Jewish writers are part of a dysfunctional family or what Jacobson calls 'my dysfunction' as an 'English Jew'. Some survive the family, such as Baron, Bernard Kops, Feinstein, Rubens, Sinclair and Wesker, and some fall by the wayside such as Camberton, Charles, Finn, Smith and Glanville. Evidence of such dysfunction is supplied in abundance by Glanville, who, at the height of the 'new wave' of British-Jewish literature, in December 1958, began a series of interviews in the *Jewish Chronicle* with an emerging group of poets, dramatists and novelists under the heading 'Young Jewish Writers and the Community'. The writers interviewed were Dannie Abse, Baron, Kops, Wolf Mankowitz, Peter

Shaffer and Wesker. All refused any engagement with the established British-Jewish community and (with Glanville's prompting) referred instead to Arthur Koestler's oft-stated belief that Jews in the diaspora would either assimilate completely or immigrate to the State of Israel. Each writer rejected a mediating role between nation and community and instead spoke of an alternative East European Yiddish folk tradition (Kops and Mankowitz) or identified with British working-class culture (Baron and Wesker) or were entirely sceptical about writing in any identifiable tradition of Jewish literature (Abse and Shaffer). None thought of themselves as part of a Jewish literary community.

Only the legacy of the Holocaust could unify such disparate figures. In another set of interviews published in the early 1960s, in the *Jewish Quarterly*, Dannie Abse argued that 'Hitler has made me more of a Jew than Moses'; Baron that it was 'the master obsession of my life'; and Emanuel Litvinoff that it 'completed' his education. Such un-English preoccupations (especially in the 1960s) were summarised by the novelist Frederic Raphael, now entering his ninth decade:

My Jewishness is the Jewishness of the disillusioned diaspora Jew, the Jewishness of loneliness. ... I do not believe in salvation, either through community or religion. Thus I am not English either, for I feel myself excluded from the community of Britons. I function within it, but I am not absorbed or satisfied by it.

Raphael's early novels, *The Limits of Love* (1960) and *Lindmann* (1963), locate the Holocaust at the heart of British and European culture. In *The Limits of Love* it is the figure of Otto Kahane, a refugee from Dachau, who returns to haunt his relatives in Cricklewood, in north London, and whose presence disrupts the false equilibrium brought about by post-war suburbanisation.

For this generation of post-war writers, Jewishness was disruptive and was the opposite of Britishness. Whether it is the memory of the Holocaust, the newly formed State of Israel, proletarian Jewish life, or continental European culture, all were brought to bear to unsettle what Charles calls 'the huge, almost virgin territory of middle-class Jewish diaspora experience'. Glanville, with typical asperity, dismissed the 'new wave' of British-Jewish writing as a literature that portrays 'an East End Jewish world which no longer exists, presented in terms of a tradition which was built up and died in Eastern Europe'. The double loss, according to this lachrymose perspective, accounted for the decline of the 'new wave' of Jewish writers in Britain, in stark contrast to the American 'new wave', which included Saul Bellow, Bernard Malamud, Cynthia Ozick, Grace Paley and Roth, who transformed post-war American literature. How could British-Jewish literature possibly emerge from under this enormous shadow?

THE BRITISH-JEWISH SPECTRUM IN THE TWENTY-FIRST CENTURY

Many critics have argued that British-Jewish literature in the twenty-first century amounted to a 'stunning burst of productivity'. After all, there were around twenty-five prizes won by Jewish writers in the first two decades of the new century (see the full list at the end of this essay in Appendix 1) with, most prominently, Linda Grant awarded the Orange Prize in 2000; Harold Pinter awarded the Nobel Prize for literature in 2005; Howard Jacobson awarded the Man-Booker Prize in 2010; and Naomi Alderman awarded the Baileys Prize in 2017. Going in and out of Britishness and Jewishness in the new century could mean travelling outwardly to Europe or Israel/Palestine or the United States or inwardly exploring the genealogy and imagined realities of Jewish experience in the United Kingdom. It could also mean writing fictionalised memoirs, conventional family romances, or experimental novels. None of these subjects or literary forms are a complete break from the past but the confidence and knowingness of this younger generation – following the 'Jews with attitude' in the 1990s – is often quite new.

The novel that did most to revitalise British-Jewish fiction in our new century is Naomi Alderman's *Disobedience* (2006) which, for a first novel, was showered with prizes, a host of enthusiastic reviews, and in 2017 was turned into a feature film. It highlighted a generational change in British-Jewish writing and also anticipated increased imaginative involvement (memoir, fiction, visual media) with the global ultra-Orthodox community. By evoking a set of religious values that are counter-modern, Alderman has changed the historic expectations associated with the Jewish novel in Britain going back to the first half of the nineteenth century. The earliest Jewish writers explained to a wider nation that Jews were potentially good, modern citizens in their quest for full political and civil rights. Citizenship, inevitably, meant integration and conformity to the dominant values of society – family, community, entrepreneurship, religious practice in private – which resulted, as Gerda Charles noted, in increased suburbanisation and acculturation. Although there are many different kinds of Jewish writing, one strand of this literature, lauded by the community, broadly conformed to this apologetic tradition. But, in defiance of the community, such apologetics were always open to revolt – as Glanville (one of many) demonstrated.

Up until the publication of *Disobedience*, the common way for Jewish writers to avoid the myth of the 'good Jew', or model citizen, was either to satirise or debunk Jewish suburbanisation, focus on those who had been left out of the narrative of liberal self-improvement – mainly those too poor or old or traumatised to move – or write about Jewish experience outside of the borders of Britishness. *Disobedience* changes the narrative by focusing on what has been aptly called by the scholar Nadia Valman the 'repressed other' of acculturated British-Jews, the 'insular unclassed world of ultra-Orthodoxy'. By definition, orthodoxy is not concerned with the demands of modernity as its values prohibit acculturation and are indifferent to suburbanisation. Above all, it has no need to debate the nature of 'Jewish identity'. Alderman's literary world, unlike previous preoccupations, is neither haunted by the legacy of the Holocaust, nor is it particularly Zionist (regarded as a secular form of nationalism), nor is it overly concerned with antisemitism. Jewish identity in *Disobedience* is not part of a genealogy that relates back to supposed 'ghettoisation' in Britain or Eastern Europe. There is no debate about whether one is British or Jewish as Orthodox Jews are undeniably a product of halacha, rabbinic thought, and the reading of the Torah in Hendon.

One must go back to Aguilar's evocation of the Hebrew Bible, as the precursor of English Protestantism, to find Judaism treated with such seriousness in the novel form. By the time of Zangwill's *Children of the Ghetto* (1892), orthodoxy was condemned as rigid and unbending, particularly with regard to its female characters. While this may also be true of *Disobedience*, the major difference is that the New York-based female protagonist, Ronit Krushka, the daughter of the communal rabbi, is not a passive victim of orthodoxy. Her lesbianism is as natural and authentic as her Jewishness and her voice is as attractive and as compelling as any Smart Alec or Smart Alice. At times she is so close to her male predecessors that she echoes Philip Roth's words almost verbatim. In America, there is:

> A vast participation in the cultural and intellectual life of the country of people who want to talk about, write about, think about Jewish things … You don't get that here [in Britain]. It's as though Jews in this country have made an *investment* in silence. There's a vicious circle here, in which the Jewish fear of being noticed and natural British reticence interact. … Which bothers me, because while I have given up being Orthodox, I can't give up being a Jew. I'm stuck with it.

Ronit's ire is not aimed at orthodox Judaism but at the silence and invisibility of British Jews in general. In New York, her life is 'full of noise'. But this perspective has been heard before. Ronit is not the first literary character to say this, not even the first 'Hendonite', as that accolade goes to many of the protagonists in Clive Sinclair's early stories and novels. Even Ronit's lesbian identity, and focus on female desire, follows a long British-Jewish tradition that goes back at least to the fiction and poetry of Amy Levy (1861–89) and family romances of Naomi Jacob

(1884–1964). But where *Disobedience* is quite new is in marginalising and appropriating the masculine voice which had dominated Jewish literature in Britain and America for most of the nineteenth and twentieth centuries. There were, of course, many exceptions to this rule; notably, in recent times, Jenny Diski, Elaine Feinstein and Linda Grant. But by removing the context of a thrusting Jewish modernity, and introducing a wholly other set of values, Alderman enables her female characters to gain freedom (even when they choose to be invisible) in a world which demarcates masculinity and femininity.

These alternative Judaic values take the form of wise and witty Talmudic sayings at the start of chapters engaging with the nature of happiness, the meaning of the Sabbath, and the importance of free will or the necessity to disobey. They add both to a sense of authenticity and, equally, reinforce the divided narrative between a female believer (Esti) and non-believer (Ronit). The Judaic texts challenge the imagination as the sole purveyor of fictive truth and reinforce a desire for what David Shields has called 'reality hunger'. By this, Shields means a desire by the contemporary reader for the authentic, 'real', historic and lived, rather than imagined truth. There is an irony here as from an Orthodox Jewish perspective fiction *is* nothing more than lies. Perhaps that is why such controversial memoirs as Reva Mann's *The Rabbi's Daughter: A True Story of Sex, Drugs and Orthodoxy* (2007), published soon after *Disobedience,* are read next to Alderman's novel. In contrast, the Orthodox Jewish world invoked in Zoë Heller's *The Believers* (2008) does not have the ring of truth as it is evoked through secular eyes as one of several possible identities. The rabbi's daughters in Alderman's novel and Mann's memoir assert that Orthodox Judaism ought to be as much a part of the body as the soul so as to conform to woman's rounded experience and not just man's. Such is the power of female desire, which disrupts both the novel form and Orthodox Judaism.

After her accomplished and understated *Daughters of Jerusalem* (2003), Charlotte Mendelson's *When We Were Bad* (2007) evokes a liberal, cosmopolitan, matriarchal Judaism in stark contrast to Alderman. In line with convention, *When We Were Bad* explores, ambitiously, the centuries-old conundrum which has preoccupied the Jewish imagination in Britain for over two centuries. Mendelson wants to understand:

> What it's like to be Jewish in England – how weird it is, and how different to being Jewish in America or being non-Jewish in England. It's a particularly odd experience. Whatever kind of Jew you are – Orthodox, liberal, practicing, non-practicing – you are never quite fully English, even in in multicultural, cosmopolitan, twenty-first-century London. England is the least Jewish country in the world.

Or, as the purported victim of English antisemitism – the protagonist in Roth's novel *Deception* (1990) – argues: 'I have never felt more misplaced in *any* country than in England.' But the problem with seeing England or Britain as the opposite of Jewishness ('whatever kind of Jew you are') is that it lacks authenticity. That is fine if you are writing a deliberately inauthentic fiction but, if you are striving for realism, as Mendelson is, then Jewishness has to be more than not-English. Ironically, the liberal hypocrisy of Rabbi Claudia Rubin, the matriarch of the novel, could not have been more English. But, as the reviewer in *JR* (July 2007) notes, Rubin is not Jewish enough: 'There are many jarring aspects of the religious elements in the book.' No wonder, after this novel, Mendelson has chosen to codify her characters in *Almost English* (2013) as Central European, much like Brookner did in her fictions. In that way, Mendelson does not need to satisfy the 'reality hunger' of her Jewish readers.

The most significant male writer of this new generation is undoubtedly Jeremy Gavron, who published two path-breaking novels, *The Book of Israel* (2002) and *An Acre of Barren Ground* (2005). More recently, he has published a memoir, *A Woman on the Edge of Time: A Son's Search for his Mother* (2015), which is comparable with Gabriel Josipovici's biography of his mother, *A Life* (2001), or Linda Grant's account of her mother's dementia, *Remind Me Who I am, Again* (1998), or George Szirtes' poetic account of his mother in *A Photographer at Sixteen* (2019). All of these books are exceptional memoirs combining fascinating biographies and deeply felt Jewish or post-Holocaust histories that complement the writerly imagination. What interests me about *A Woman on the Edge of Time*, beyond its poignant narrative concerning his mother's suicide, is its implicit literary genealogy. Gavron shares a trip to Israel with the exceptional but underrated British-Jewish novelist Elisabeth Russell Taylor (1930–2020); includes snippets from a Wesker story and an interview with him as he was a close family friend; and, needless to say, his mother's own book and her writerly friends and colleagues fill the pages.

Perhaps some kind of literary heritage is inevitable given the kind of novels that Gavron has written. Both are spoof genealogies. *The Book of Israel* is a pastiche of a family saga bringing together archival and historical sources, a feature of his next novel, to portray seven generations of the fictional Dunksy (Dunn) family, originating in Lithuania in 1874 and eventually spreading to South Africa and Israel, and ending up in England in 2001. Unlike the hyper-masculinised fiction of Sinclair or Jacobson or Jonathan Wilson – or, more recently, novels by Giles Coren, Andrew Sanger and Adam Thirlwell – there is not a single, dominating and dominant masculine perspective. Voices differ, perceptions change across time and place, and the ultimate journey – taking in the First World War, the bloodlands of the Holocaust, and conflict in Israel/Palestine – is one of mundane acculturation in Britain. The chapter headings taken from the Hebrew Bible, or grandiose parodies such as 'Nuptials' or 'Hostilities', point to the gap between the messianic idealism within Judaism and the tragic realities of victimisation or, in Britain, toothless assimilation: 'mugging up' on books bought hurriedly in Golders Green so that a Seder can be held.

The last chapter, 'Circumlocution', points both to the many journeys and histories which have led the Dunn family to Britain and also to the final act of Jewish identification, the ritual of circumcision. For all of its varied voices and plural perspectives, this act of Judaising can be seen as hopelessly masculine: 'You're Jewish. Your husband is done and you want your child to be the same.' This is the case in Freedman's *Jacob's Gift*, where Jacob's circumcision is also the stimulus for narrative – the stories that make up Freedman's family history and his constant negotiations between Britishness and Jewishness. In Francesca Segal's *The Innocents* (2012), circumcision is a means of resolving conflict as it displaces 'suffering' (which Adam had caused Rachel) onto their newborn child, Kobi: 'It's going to be horrible [Kobi] but then it'll be over, I promise,' says Rachel. All three of these British writers echo Roth's *The Counterlife* (1986) where Nathan Zuckerman contrasts an England whose antisemitism turned him into an 'object … like a glass or an apple' and compares this with the anticipated circumcision of his son, which 'confirms there is an us'. That way, Zuckerman and his family can enter a collective history as subjects rather than objects. As Adam Thirlwell's debut novel, *Politics* (2006), illustrates, there is nothing more enthralling for a young male Jewish novelist than the penis – circumcised or not.

What I find especially innovative in Gavron's work is the use of intertexts (texts published elsewhere) within the novel to illustrate particular contexts or cultures. These might include a Zionist newsletter from South Africa or a series of quotations from British pulp fiction to illustrate the milieu of Jack Dunn's English public school in the 1940s. Conventional writers of British-Jewish family sagas, such as G.B. Stern or Maisie Mosco or Rosemary Friedman invariably argue that they write to counter images of 'Shylock' or 'Fagin' or 'Svengali' which still circulate in contemporary Britain. They see their fiction as rectifying these images by correcting, in their work, an imbalanced portrait of 'the Jew'. They write, in other words, to represent Jews in a favourable manner (what Roth has called, in relation to Leon Uris, 'public relations' fiction).

By providing the evidence of just how the 'swarthy Jew' was contrasted with the 'English gentleman' in British pulp fiction, Gavron can write as a subject of history rather than an object. What is more, the figures he uncovers from a subterranean British culture, such as the author Guy Thorne (1874–1923), evoke a past that is not too far from our present time. In his bestselling Edwardian novel, *When it was Dark* (1903), Thorne postulates that a 'Jewish millionaire' conspired to destroy Christianity so as to bring about global anarchy. It was a novel that the then archbishop of London advised his flock to read and is readily available today in a new imprint. Jack Dunn does not need to be turned into a 'good Jew' in response to the snippets from Thorne's fiction, which speaks for itself. Other contemporary writers, such as Natasha Solomons in her *Mr Rosenblum's List* (2010), include government information, distributed by the Board of Deputies of British Jews, on how to keep one's head down, or 'Friendly Guidance for the Aspiring Englishman'. The British-Jewish establishment has long since distributed to new Jewish immigrants 'friendly guidance' on how to be 'English'. Interest in this 'fascinating' material, as Jacobson argues, should certainly not be confined to Jewish historians as it speaks to many other refugee experiences.

Gavron forms his next novel, *An Acre of Barren Ground* (2005), around both intertexts and connections between a vast number of histories of immigration. He does this by focusing on the iconic Brick Lane in the East End of London beginning with prehistoric times and ending with migration from South East Asia. Texts are used to illustrate the multiple histories that make up Brick Lane which acts as a palimpsest with many layers resonating across centuries. The book encompasses diaries, journalism, graphic fiction, prose and poetry, and ranges from Roman conquerors to Shakespeare's sister, Huguenots, dot-com millionaires, and the seeds that grow in a post-war bomb site. There are, inevitably, a myriad of cultures in the novel but the (now forgotten) Yiddish culture of the East End is an important presence: 'A common London slang word for a thief was a *gonoph*'; 'the little English [the newly arrived] Mr Basu had learned was sprinkled with Yiddish, Urdu and Caribbean words'; '[Rudolf Rocker] a German gentile who had taught himself Yiddish' edited the *Worker's Friend*.

The close affinity between fiction-making and memoirs and genealogies is apparent when this novel is read next to Rachel Lichtenstein's and Iain Sinclair's *Rodinsky's Room* (1999) and, especially, Lichtenstein's *On Brick Lane* (2008). Gavron's reconstruction of the East End takes an epic (or at least, mock-epic) form whereas *Rodinsky's Room* and *On Brick Lane* is more detective-work and memory reconstruction. Both are in a long line of books, starting perhaps with Emmanuel Litvinoff's *Journey Through a Small Planet* (1972), that aim to tell the 'story of the disappearing Jewish East End', as Lichtenstein puts it.

The title *An Acre of Barren Ground* is a quotation from Shakespeare's *The Tempest* and is ambiguous. Does it mean that we all need some 'barren ground' to live on that belongs to us? This perspective can be seen in Tamar Yellin's essay 'A Jew in Brontëland' (2007) where she recounts her mother 'the Zionist' commenting mournfully that the Yorkshire Moors, where Yellin lives, may be 'beautiful', but 'it isn't ours'. The long historical reach and pluralism of *An Acre of Barren Ground* would suggest a diasporic interpretation as it includes many wandering people from around the globe who only live in London's East End for a short while. The *Book of Israel*, on the other hand, includes the contemporary history of Zionism and Jewish settlement in Palestine. Gavron's fiction both summarises what has gone before also blurs the lines between imaginative and historical reconstruction. In his experimentalism, Gavron echoes Simon Louvish's six-volume *The Blok Saga* (1985–2021) which incorporates Hebrew journalism and turns it into English-language fiction. Novelists such as Rubens, *The Sergeants' Tale* (2003), Jonathan Wilson, *The Palestine Affair* (2003) and Jacobson's *The Finkler Question* (2012) all engage with the history and impact of Israel/Palestine on British-Jewish life over six decades. Such is the range of subjects that the contemporary Jewish writer is not afraid to make their own.

The exception to the confidence and playfulness of the new generation of writers when it comes to the past is, inevitably, the Holocaust. Gavron makes a powerful statement about the limits of fiction in this regard when the chapter 'Esther' set in 'Riga, 1943' is merely a blank page. A few brave souls have attempted to write fiction about the Holocaust from a British-Jewish perspective – Jacobson's *Kalooki Nights* and *J: A Novel* (2014), David Baddiel's *The Secret Purposes* (2004) and Jake Wallis Simons's *The English German Girl* (2013). But it is still a history best told as a memoir, as can be seen in Eve Figes, *Tales of Innocence and Experience* (2003), Edmund de Waal, *The Hare with Amber Eyes: A Hidden Inheritance* (2011) and Hadley Freeman's *House of Glass* (2020). Dramatists such as Julia Pascal in her *Holocaust Trilogy* (1996) and Diane Samuels in her *Kindertransport* (1992), along with Pinter, *Ashes to Ashes* (1996) and Ryan Craig *The Glass Room* (2006), are also not afraid to engage with the legacy of the Holocaust. Certainly, in our new century, theatre in Britain on a range of Jewish themes – from the Oslo Accords to 'bad Jews' – has been buoyant.

But it is memoir, above all other genres, that has been in competition with imaginative literature and drama when it comes to capturing the reality of Jewish life in Britain and beyond. All of the novels and plays reflecting on the Holocaust incorporate historical material to gain authenticity. On the other hand, the best memoirs are nothing if not acts of the authorial imagination. No longer is an all-encompassing British-Jewish literature necessarily confined to a single form or genre but, instead, can mix up the way it recounts its story in any one book or play. British-Jewish experience is complicated and many of the new generation recognise this by writing books or plays that acknowledge rather than belittle the complexity of this experience.

2016: THE CENTRE CANNOT HOLD

There was an extraordinary explosion of British-Jewish fiction, drama, poetry, and memoir in the first decade of our new century. But this century has already undergone dramatic changes. In 2016 the United Kingdom voted to leave the European Union, Donald Trump was elected as president of the USA, and, in 2019, a global pandemic has changed the world permanently in ways that we cannot yet even imagine. By 2016 it was clear that many of the new-generation writers in that initial 2003 list were publishing fiction of Jewish interest infrequently or not at all.

It is the older generation – writers such as David Baddiel, Esther Freud, Linda Grant, Howard Jacobson, Gabriel Josipovici, Deborah Levy, Patrick Marber, William Sutcliffe and Jonathan Wilson – who are most prominent currently and have published some of their best work in the past decade. There are exceptions, of course, with a number of significant 'survivors' from the newer generation still publishing regularly but not always on Jewish themes. These include Naomi Alderman, Jeremy Gavron, Charlotte Mendelson, Francesca Segal, Natasha Solomons and Adam Thirlwell. Many of the older generation have died out in the past decade – Dannie Abse, Jenny Diski, Emanuel Litvinoff, Elaine Feinstein, Clive Sinclair, Arnold Wesker – and it will be soon only the younger generation who will make up the British-Jewish literary dysfunctional family.

But, in our present moment, it is noticeable that those Jewish writers who have engaged with the big issues in our recent times – Brexit, Trump, Jeremy Corbyn, Covid-19 – have all come from the older generation: Jacobson in his Trumpian satire *Pussy* (2017), Grant on Brexit in her important novel, *A Stranger City* (2019), and Tom Stoppard in his one self-proclaimed 'Jewish play' (following Mike Leigh), *Leopoldstadt* (2020), which relates modern Austrian history to the xenophobia and nationalism of the present. Michael Rosen has recently published a moving account of his own brush with death, *Many Different Kinds of Love: A Story of Life, Death, and the NHS* (2021). Baddiel, in his *Jews Don't Count* (2021), comes closest to understanding current 'progressive' exclusion of Jewish experience in relation to the questions of racism, minority status and refugee experience. Where once British-Jewish literature was seen as part of a larger multicultural ethos, as Baddiel makes clear, it is now omitted from the canon of new 'ethnic' literatures. The optimism and self-confidence felt at the beginning of our new century by younger novelists, dramatists, and poets, has clearly dissipated in the past decade – and for good reason. More worrying still, where are the dramatists, poets, and novelists today who are under 40?

The answer to this question is complicated and has much to do with the glo-balisation of publishing and the difficulties of all young writers – Jewish and non-Jewish – finding a publisher who is willing to invest in new talent, especially at a time when Jews are not considered fashionable. But, more optimistically, we can look elsewhere for imaginative accounts of British Jews such as UK television – *Grandma's House* by Simon Amstell and Dan Swimer, the plays of Steven Poliakoff, Robert Popper's *Friday Night Dinner* – are all good current examples. Globally Jewish subjects can be found prominently online via numer-ous TV shows – *Shtisel, Unorthodox, The Marvellous Mrs Maisel, Schitt's Creek, My Unorthodox Life* – and they have a large enough audience to generate many series. But whether the ubiquity of mass media means that Jewish writers will have to tell a more global story or continue with local histories is as yet unknown. The broadcasting and media careers of Ronald Harwood, Jacobson, Pinter, Raphael, and Jack Rosenthal have obviously complemented their imaginative work. Perhaps this is the future? But one can predict everything apart from the future. What I do know is that British-Jewish literature has existed for over two centuries and there are plenty of reasons to be optimistic over the past two dec-ades. British-Jews driven by their imaginations will continue to find a way to recount their experience. One way will undoubtedly be on the page and stage, but the large and small screen will also be part of a rich tapestry of creativity.

APPENDIX 1: JEWISH WINNERS OF LITERARY PRIZES 2000–20

2000: Linda Grant, *When I Lived in Modern Times*, Orange Prize for Fiction; Howard Jacobson, *The Mighty Walzer*, Jewish Quarterly-Wingate Prize.

2001: Esther Morgan, *Beyond Calling Distance*, Jerwood Aldeburgh First Collection Prize.

2002: James Lasdun, *The Horned Man*, a *New York Times* Notable Book of the Year.

2003: Charlotte Mendelson, *Daughters of Jerusalem*, John Llewellyn Rhys Prize; Jeremy Gavron, *Book of Israel*, Encore Award; Adam Thirwell, *Politics*, Betty Trask Award and Granta Best of Young British Writers.

2004: Charlotte Mendelson, *Daughters of Jerusalem*, Somerset Maugham Award.

2005: Harold Pinter awarded the Nobel Prize for literature.

2006: Naomi Alderman, *Disobedience*, Orange Award for New Writers; Tamar Yellin, *The Genizah at the House of Shepher*, Sami Rohr Prize for Jewish Literature and the Harold U. Ribalow Prize.

2007: Howard Jacobson, *Kalooki Nights*, Jewish Quarterly-Wingate Prize.

2008: Adam Thirlwell, *Miss Herbert*, Somerset Maugham Award.
2009: Zoë Heller, *The Believers*, *Jewish Quarterly*-Wingate Prize.
2010: Howard Jacobson, *The Finkler Question*, Man-Booker Prize.
2012: Francesca Segal, *The Innocents*, Costa Prize.
2013: Francesca Segal, *The Innocents*, Betty Trask Award and the Sami Rohr
      Prize for Jewish Literature; William Sutcliffe, *The Wall*, Palestine Book Award;
      Naomi Alderman and Adam Thirlwell, Granta Best of Young British Writers.
2015: Adam Thirlwell, *Lurid & Cute*, E.M. Forster Award.
2017: Naomi Alderman, *The Power*, Baileys Prize for Fiction.
2018: Eli Goldstone, *Strange Heart Beating*, Betty Trask Award.
2020: Linda Grant, *A Stranger City*, *Jewish Quarterly*-Wingate Prize.

APPENDIX 2: BIBLIOGRAPHY

This essay could not have been written without some important books, articles, reviews and interviews by a significant number of critics and academics, which I list below. But I do want to thank David Herman, in particular, who has engaged with contemporary British-Jewish novelists and dramatists more than anyone else. His reviews and interviews can be found, mainly, in *JR*, *Jewish Quarterly* and the *Jewish Chronicle*, but also in the *TLS*, *Prospect*, *New Statesman*, *Salmagundi*, and *PN Review*. His account of contemporary British-Jewish literature differs from mine, but he was generous enough to share his personal chronology of the past twenty years, which has helped to shape my thinking.

I also want to thank Ruth Gilbert, whose *Writing Jewish: Contemporary British-Jewish Literature* (Palgrave, 2013) is an essential starting point for this topic to which I am indebted. The other influential starting point is 'Anglo-Jewish Literature Raises its Voice', by Donald Weber, which was published online in JBooks in 2007 (available at www.jbooks.com/interviews/index/IP_Weber_English.htm). My colleague David Brauner has published three important books, *Post-War Jewish Fiction: Ambivalence, Self-Explanation and Transatlantic Connections* (Palgrave, 2001); *Howard Jacobson* (Manchester University Press, 2020); and, with Axel Stähler, the co-edited *The Edinburgh Companion to Modern Jewish Fiction* (Edinburgh University Press, 2015). Stähler has also co-edited with Sue Vice *Writing Jews and Jewishness in Contemporary Britain*, a special issue of *European Judaism*, vol. 47, no. 2 (2014). Both Stähler and Vice have published many interesting books and articles on British-Jewish and Holocaust literature. Particularly helpful for this essay was Stähler's 'Between or Beyond? Jewish British Short Stories in English since the 1970s', and Vice's 'British-Jewish Writing in the

Post-2016 Era: Tom Stoppard, Linda Grant and Howard Jacobson', both published online in *Humanities* (September 2020) on 'Contemporary British-Jewish Literature, 1970-2020' (available at www.mdpi.com/journal/humanities/special_issues/british_jewish). I also learned a great deal from Karen Skinazi's *Women of Valor* (Rutgers University Press, 2018) in relation to the increased interest in Orthodox Jewish women in our new century.

The essay also builds on my own work, namely my edited *Contemporary Jewish Writing in Britain and Ireland: An Anthology* (Nebraska University Press, 1998), a book on Muriel Spark, an essay on British-Jewish Literature in Laura Marcus and Peter Nicholls (eds.), *The Cambridge History of Twentieth-Century English Literature* (Cambridge University Press, 2005), and an essay on 'Contemporary Jewish Writing in Britain' in Vivian Liska and Thomas Nolden (eds.), *Contemporary Jewish Writing in Europe: A Guide* (Indiana University Press, 2008). I had the good sense to commission Nadia Valman on 'Jewish Fictions' for my co-edited (with Peter Boxall), *The Oxford History of the Novel in English: British and Irish Fiction Since 1940* (Oxford University Press, 2016). I am particularly indebted to this essay and all of Valman's pathbreaking scholarship most recently on the literature of the East End of London.

Most of this essay has been on the novel with some reference to key dramatists and poets. For more on contemporary British-Jewish poetry, see Peter Lawson (ed.), *Passionate Renewal: Jewish Poetry in Britain Since 1945: An Anthology* (Five Leaves Publications, 2001), and his book, *Anglo-Jewish Poetry from Isaac Rosenberg to Elaine Feinstein* (Vallentine Mitchell, 2006). *A Companion to British-Jewish Theatre Since the 1950s* (Methuen, 2021) edited by Jeanette R. Malkin, Eckart Voigts and Sarah Jane Ablett was yet to be published at the time of going to press but is expected to be a definitive book on British-Jewish drama.

It should be clear from the references to the critical work above that there is a vibrant critical and scholarly community in Britain that addresses British-Jewish literature in a wide variety of forms. The abundance of imaginative literature has been my primary inspiration. But my guide has been the scholarly work which tries to make sense of the many books, plays, films and TV shows that continue to this day. When I first started writing on British-Jewish literature as an isolated postgraduate student, more than three decades ago, I had no idea how creative, enjoyable and intellectually stimulating this area was to become. What a pleasure it is to share my ideas with such a wide community.

FROM THE *JR* ARCHIVE

'THE TEXTLINE', BY HELGA ABRAHAM

'The Textline' featured in the January 2013 issue of JR. *Helga Abraham talked to the Israeli writer Amos Oz and his daughter, the historian Fania Oz-Salzberger, about their love of words and how they created a new theory of the Jewish people in their book,* Jews and Words, *which was published by Yale University Press in 2012.*

Amos Oz was an Israeli writer, novelist and journalist and regarded as one of Israel's most prolific and respected intellectuals. He died in December 2018.

Fania Oz-Salzberger is professor of history at the University of Haifa School of Law and the Haifa Centre for German and European Studies.

Helga Abraham grew up in London and lives in Jerusalem. She is a freelance journalist and translator with a background in broadcasting.

Amos Oz was born in Jerusalem, ran away to a kibbutz at the age of 14, and lives today in the Negev town of Arad. His daughter Fania Oz-Salzberger lives in Haifa, where she is a professor of history at Haifa University. We meet in Oz's apartment in north Tel Aviv, which, like his house in Arad, is lined with books.

While both father and daughter exude the same warmth, charm and simplicity, their different temperaments become quickly apparent: the father is the poetic writer, the daughter the analytical intellect; he is quiet and reserved, she bubbly and outgoing, and as much as the novelist is eloquent, the historian is articulate. As they sit side by side – bantering, joking, concurring, arguing and sometimes correcting each other – they epitomise, for me, two generations of 'thinking' and involved Israeli sabras.

★★★

When novelist Amos Oz was a small child, his ambition was to become, not a writer, but a book. This was not simply due to his love of books. 'It was from fear,' he says. 'When I was a little boy in Jerusalem, we lived in the shadow both of the Holocaust and of an impending second Holocaust for there was great fear that when the British pulled out of Palestine, millions of Arabs would come and strangle us. I realised then that not every boy grows up to be a man but if I became a book I would survive in some faraway library.'

Pertinently Oz, Israel's elder man of letters and serial prizewinner, has now co-authored together with his daughter, historian Fania Oz-Salzberger, a book, *Jews and Words*, which is an elegy to the quintessential surviving book – the Bible – to the literary corpus it engendered, to its eloquent language and accompanying tradition of interpreting, reinterpreting, arguing and talking. Taking this one step further, the father-daughter team put forward the somewhat revolutionary thesis that it is words and the transmission of an ancient literary tradition which has kept the Jews together, in a textline rather than bloodline.

Although the authors wrote their new book in English – both possess perfect command of the English language – they say that they were not aiming specifically at a diaspora public. 'We did not write the book for Jews or non-Jews, the Diaspora or Israel,' says Oz, 'We wrote it for lovers of books and lovers of words.' *Jews and Words* has already sold out in the US and is due to come out shortly in Hebrew, German, French, Dutch and Italian, possibly even Chinese.

Oz's love of books began before he could even read, with the bedtime stories his parents read to him and their love of words: 'They would point out the similarity between two different words or how the tiniest twist could make a word change its meaning completely. So I became infatuated, not just with stories, but with the words themselves.' To date, Oz's prolific literary output spans 19 novels, 8 works of nonfiction and countless essays and articles. A supreme intellectual, propelled by curiosity, he owns a personal library of 8,000 books.

In the Oz family – as in the bigger tribal family – love of words has been a central motif running from generation to generation. Oz's grandfather, Alexander Klausner, wrote Zionist poetry, his great-uncle Joseph Klausner was a renowned scholar who owned a collection of 20,000 books, his father was a librarian and book collector, his mother a storyteller, his daughter Fania has written two works of non-fiction, *Translating the Enlightenment* and *Israelis in Berlin*, his youngest daughter Galia is a successful writer of children's books, and his son Daniel is about to publish his second volume of poetry in Hebrew.

Fania recalls that her first toys were books and her earliest memories were in words. 'When you are very young,' she says, 'there is a sensuality carved onto texts and letters that remains with you all your life.' Today she finds a similar sensuality in the Kindle and the iPad: 'I love the touch of these sleek, metallic, super-lightweight books … even the little click of turning the pages electronically is sensual.' Her father demurs: 'I like the object, I like to hold it and write little notes in the margin.' While the historian contributed the cutting-edge analogies that pepper the book (e.g. 'tablet to tablet, scroll to scroll') and likes to describe the internet as 'a wonderful maze of meaning in a very talmudic space,' the novelist is less enthusiastic: 'I think the internet is an addiction and I try to avoid addictions in my life.'

When asked how the two worked together on the book, Oz answers, 'I can answer in two words; we talked.' The transition from talking to writing may have been 'smooth and joyful', but there were, admits Fania, quite a few disagreements along the way. 'I am a historian and I am strict about fact-finding and less patient with generalisations. My co-author, in contrast, loves generalisations. So I made sure that we backed what we said with facts and sources as much as possible, and I brought in most of the footnotes.' Disagreements aside, both of them view the joint venture in a positive light: 'We were very good friends before and we are even better friends now,' says Oz. 'It's good family therapy to write a book together,' says Fania.

Both father and daughter are avowed secularists. In *Jews and Words* they define themselves as the 'Atheists of the Book', but the fact of being secular, they say, does not mean abandoning the ancient Jewish texts. 'As a secular Jew, I feel a legitimate heir to the Jewish library,' says Oz. Not only an heir but a huge fan, for this supremely unreligious writer describes the Bible as 'the greatest book I have ever read' and, in *Jews and Words*, accords it boundless superlatives such as 'breathtaking', 'magnificent', 'palatial'.

'The Bible is in my veins,' says Oz, 'I know sections by heart from my childhood and I read a chapter every morning of my life … over and over again.' Oz finds inspiration for his own writing in the 'poetic and algebraic quality of biblical narration', and although he admires the beauty of the King James translation, he says it does not always reflect the original Hebrew. 'Take the fifth commandment. The Hebrew says 'lo tirtzach/do not murder'; the English says 'do not kill'. There is not the slightest etymological proximity between 'murder' and 'kill'; they are two different concepts entirely.'

The historian adds: 'This is a mistranslation with a deep moral meaning, which we think is a Christian input, for it can be interpreted as saying that all killing is bad, even in self-defence.'

If the authors have an axe to grind, it is within the Jewish world itself and within the ever-intensifying Orthodox vs secular debate. Indeed, their book can be seen as entering into the fray with gusto on behalf of the secular side. 'Our book is political in the sense that we are reclaiming our ancestry and our legacy from the smug sort of Jewish Orthodoxy,' says Fania. As to why this should be necessary, Oz explains: 'In the most horrible Jewish tradition, some Orthodox tried to inflict guilt on the secular with accusations such as 'your Judaism is not Judaism' and 'ours is the only genuine Judaism', so now we are saying that this heritage belongs also to us, and perhaps even more so because we have a broader perspective.'

Apparently, the right of secular Jewry to comment on biblical texts is not a given. Fania recounts how, in a recent review of *Jews and Words*, a prominent American rabbi stated that the authors could not do as they pleased with the Bible and the Talmud and that secular Jews, anyway, are unable to maintain the Jewish tradition because they are like cut flowers in a vase.

To this Oz quips: 'They call us cut flowers and I call them dried flowers.' Fania: 'They say that we do not understand the Bible and are not entitled to read it selectively.'

On this point, father and daughter are equally passionate and proudly remark – in a nudge to the American rabbi – that, despite five generations of secularism in their family, they have maintained a rich Jewish library and love of its moral legacy. While theirs has been an unbroken chain of continuity, they are in many ways reflecting, with their new book, the greater phenomenon of secular Israelis returning to ancient sources. As they note in the book, 'there are today more Bible-wise atheists in Israel than anywhere else.' The historian points out that secular Israelis 'are not only returning to the Bible with a vengeance, they are studying the Talmud, and rock groups in Tel Aviv are setting medieval Sephardi poets to music. It is a veritable renaissance of words!'

As to the age-old question of what defines Jewish identity, Oz does not dispute the role of faith. 'We do not claim that religion is irrelevant, heaven forbid,' he says. 'We are simply saying that it is not exclusive and is not the only way to be Jewish.' And while, for him and his daughter, the Hebrew language and the fact of living in Israel are crucial components of their Jewish identity, it is the tradition of the Jewish texts and scholarship which they say constitutes the central link to their Jewish heritage. And Amos Oz goes even further, stating adamantly: 'If Jews lose their rapport with the texts, they will eventually be cut off from Jewish continuity.'

Anita Brookner, 1986. (Peter Jordan / Alamy Stock Photo)

Harold Pinter (right) and William Friedkin on the set of *The Birthday Party*, 1968. (Everett Collection / Alamy Stock Photo)

Howard Jacobson at home in central
London, 2019. (Rob Greig)

Israel Zangwill, *c.* 1905.
(Everett Collection)

Bernice Rubens at home in Hampstead, London, 1995. (Steve Speller / Alamy Stock Photo)

Frederic Raphael, 2016. (David Levenson / Getty Images)

Naomi Alderman, 2017. (Lorenzo Dalberto / Alamy Stock Photo)

Rachel McAdams (left) and Rachel Weisz in *Disobedience*, 2017. (TCD / Prod. DB / Alamy Stock Photo)

Jeremy Gavron, 2016. (Gary Doak / Alamy Stock Photo)

Linda Grant, 2008. (Reuters / Alamy Stock Photo)

Sit and Shiver by Steven Berkoff at the Hackney Empire, London, 2007. Berkoff as Lionel. (Sheila Burnett / ArenaPAL)

One Jewish Boy by Stephen Laughton at Trafalgar Studios, London, 2020. With Robert Neumark-Jones and Asha Reid. (Pamela Raith Photography)

Caroline, Or Change by Tony Kushner at the Playhouse Theatre, London, 2018. With Sharon D. Clarke as Caroline Thibodeaux and Ako Mitchell (both centre). (Helen Maybanks / ArenaPAL)

Bad Jews by Joshua Harmon at the Theatre Royal Haymarket, London, 2016. With Ilan Goodman (left) as Liam, Ailsa Joy (centre) as Daphna, Antonia Kinlay as Melody and Jos Slovick as Jonah. (Nobby Clark / ArenaPAL)

The Holy Rosenbergs by Ryan Craig at the Cottesloe at the National Theatre, London, 2011. With Henry Goodman (left) as David, Susannah Wise (far end of table) as Ruth, Tilly Tremayne as Lesley and Paul Freeman as Saul. (Johan Persson/ArenaPAL)

Dr Korczak's Example by David Greig at St John's Church, Edinburgh, as part of the Just festival, 2018. With Fraser Macrae and Lianne Harris. (Steven Scott Taylor / Alamy Stock Photo)

FROM THE *JR* ARCHIVE

'LITERARY COCAINE LACED WITH OLD-FASHIONED SEXISM', BY LINDA GRANT

The July 2015 issue of JR *marked the centenary of the birth of the great American writer Saul Bellow with a piece by novelist Linda Grant. In the article, she asked whether Bellow's writing still has the ability to touch a nerve today?*

Linda Grant is a novelist and journalist. She is the author of eight novels, including When I Lived in Modern Times *(2000), which won the Orange Prize for Fiction, and* The Clothes on Their Backs *(2008), which was shortlisted for the Man Booker Prize and won the South Bank Show award in the literature category. Grant was appointed a Fellow of the Royal Society of Literature in 2014.*

A hundred years since the birth of Saul Bellow, and ten years since the morning I heard the news of his death on the radio and screamed aloud in rage and sorrow – howled because he was no longer in the world – critics and readers are starting to ask, inevitably, was he worth it? Will his reputation survive? Nothing withers as fast as the voice of a generation. Even while he was still writing, some regarded Bellow as an embarrassing relic of an era in which writing symbolised the all-male authorial voice, politics was defined in reaction to and against the squabbles of the pre-war American left and post-war McCarthyism, and women were characterised as ball-breaking bitches or heavily perfumed jezebels.

I came to Bellow quite late. I had tried to read Herzog in my teens but was snagged on the jacket description of the hero as a 'novelist manqué'. I didn't know what the word meant and it wasn't in my dictionary. The trials of divorced middle-aged men in Chicago were out of the zone of what Amazon reviewers call 'relatability'. I gave up. Not until the 1990s did I get round to reading *The Adventures of Augie March*, which was probably where I should have started in the first place.

I've never taken cocaine, but I imagine that its effect was like that of reading *Augie*. An exhilarating ride. *Augie* was published when Bellow was in his late 30s yet it still seems a youthful novel. He based it on an old friend who would cry, while playing cards, 'I gotta scheme!' It revelled in America, in being an American, in the chaos and vitality of the great cities; it had none of the pinched, ironic charm of the contemporary English novel, or its misanthropy. I adored Bellow because he fulfilled the Jew in me, the Jew that in English society tries to assimilate and pass.

From *Augie March* I went on to *Humboldt's Gift*. It felt like a blood transfusion. Bellow had become a conservative, but in his hands that didn't matter because instead of squatting on the territory of 'writer of conscience', which is easy – anyone can sign a petition – he was a 'writer of consciousness'.

As I wrote at the time of his death, such an individual is 'forever conflicted by the competing demands of the great cities, the individual's urge to survival against all odds and his equal need for love and some kind of penetrating understanding of what there was of significance beyond all the racket and racketeering'.

Bellow stood against capitalism not as an economic system but against its rapacious tendency to stunt the imagination and the intellect. The shadow cast over him was that of his successful businessman brother, who thought him a fool for thinking too much; Saul never even owned his own home.

The other reason Bellow's novels send the sap rising is language. Immigrants, the writers who know the streets, reinvigorate the over-worked prose that descends down from Henry James. Bellow knew Yiddish so well he became Isaac Bashevis Singer's first translator, and the salt of Yiddish and the demotic of the streets made the American novel the powerhouse of the English language. He didn't just know street slang, mobsters, Jewish mothers, struggling immigrants but college professors, failed poets, raddled intellectuals.

I think of Bellow as a sexist and Roth as a misogynist. No room here to go into why, but Bellow simply seems a man of his times – an old-fashioned era before the women's movement when women existed to be fucked, then possibly married, and then certainly divorced. Say what you like about Henry James' stifled personal life, he could create fictional women. When you pick up a Bellow, you must accept that it's the male psyche that is to be taken as the universal. Both his biographers, James Atlas, and now Zachary Leader, have no trouble conceding he wasn't the world's nicest guy, particularly in his relationships with women. He used other people's lives ruthlessly in his fiction, but that can't matter when we judge his work. The question is whether it will come to feel dated, a relic of times long past. And whether his themes – America as crucible of both greed and energy – will survive that country's slow leak as a world power. I wonder if writers of colour (such as Toni Morrison) might come to be more to the taste of the new century.

The test of his longevity will be if he comes to be read more or less solely in the universities. Posterity is cruel. Reputations fail often a week after the obituary notices. Who now reads John Dos Passos for pleasure? Even Ernest Hemingway is seen as old hat. Bellow's genius was to remind you that you were alive, that being alive was a hell of a thing, that 'I want, I want, I want', the primal scream, was in the nature of men and women. You know you are alive when you are reading him, and that the world he writes about is a living place, not because of research or lyrical prose but because he seems to be mainlining reality. I hope that it's the life force that saves him – the quality of conveying what it is to live, because in that he is unsurpassed.

BEING COMFORTABLE WITH THE UNCOMFORTABLE: TWENTY YEARS OF JEWISH THEATRE

JUDI HERMAN

Two people are having a heated dispute. Finally, they agree to go to a renowned rabbi for a judgement. The first carefully outlines their side of the argument. The rabbi listens intently and eventually says, 'My friend, you are right.' The disputant goes away satisfied. Later in the day, the other party arrives and tells the rabbi their side of the issue. The rabbi again listens carefully, impressed with the arguments, and replies after some thought, 'You are right.' Later, the rabbi's wife, who overheard the rabbi's conversations with both parties, says to him, 'Shmuel, you told both of them they were right, surely this cannot be?' To which the rabbi replies, 'And you are right too!'

The dispute might just as well have been over the question of 'what is Jewish theatre?' and considering that Jewish theatre encompasses performers, directors, authors, producers, venues and audiences, the only consensus is that there is no consensus. So perhaps then, everyone is right – or, as theatre critic Michael Billington wondered in a *Guardian* column back in 2012, 'is there, in fact, such a thing as a Jewish theatrical identity? Or are there simply a lot of talented writers who are Jews?'

The finer points of debate nowadays are largely confined to literary criticism, media studies or symposia in which the contested concept of Jewish theatre stubbornly defies precise definition. Is it theatre by Jews? For Jews? About Jews?

What an opportunity this offers for no end of contemporary *midrashim* and academic papers connecting new Jewish realities and the text. But it is not just the long history of disputation carried into the contemporary period that has fuelled the debate over the last twenty years.

This has been a time of extraordinary cultural change, including the continued wavering of religious adherence, with even more Jews identifying as secular or cultural rather than belonging to any of the religious streams of Judaism; the greater acceptance of lesbian, gay, bisexual, transgender and queer or questioning (LGBTQ+) rights; and technology-driven social media fuelling behaviours and attitudes that arise with strong loyalty to a social grouping.

While Israel continues to be a central component in Jewish identity, its nature and strength have been changing along with changes in individual experiences and our collective agenda. Even the Holocaust is now a staple of popular fiction and theatre. The preoccupations of playwrights, the role of Jewish characters within theatrical representations and the perspective of both the Jew and the non-Jew in the audience gazing at the spectacle have changed dramatically over the past twenty years.

Embarking on this essay, I was gratified to discover that, over the two decades of its existence, the various articles, interviews and reviews on theatre and its practitioners published in *JR* provide a real feel for the changing scope and nature of the theatrical landscape, encompassing all the various definitions of Jewish theatre. Over two decades, the magazine has been championing the diversity of the Jewish experience in the UK and uncovering the wealth of activity of Jewish interest around the world. How, in that time, has theatre of Jewish interest evolved, and been perceived to have evolved, with everyone now a critic via social media?

Fortunately, there has been a trend of late in academia for an emphasis on performance rather than drama and this opens the way for seeing Jewish theatre as any theatre of 'Jewish interest'. And that certainly includes theatre not created by Jewish artists. Such a definition also shifts the perspective from the author, the script or the actor to the interpretive meaning attached to performance by the audience – and no less by the theatre critic or journalist.

We all experience a piece of theatre from our own perspective. Jews have been adept over the centuries at navigating between the culture of their heritage and cultural acquisitions, but the last twenty years has seen us all much more open to, and aware of, our own 'acculturated understanding', the way we adapt to and adopt common cultural values around us. The original (Jewish) culture remains but is somewhat changed by the process.

So this essay gazes in more detail at the shifting perspectives of Jewish theatre as seen by readers (or putative readers) of, and writers for, *JR*. That gaze takes in the ever-changing Jewish voice on stage and re-appraises authors who have focused on Jewish themes and those whose 'Jewishness' is freshly evaluated in revivals. It considers writers and directors who, whatever they say, are deemed by us, the viewers, to bring a uniquely Jewish scrutiny to their work. There's an inevitable focus on what might have been reasonably within the purview of *JR* and a necessary emphasis on the UK scene, which of course encompasses international work of Jewish interest, whether in visiting productions or those first staged in the UK. A mere chronological perspective, however, does not do justice to the debate and what follows is as kaleidoscopic as the topic. I apologise in advance for all the wonderful – and dreadful – plays of which I make no mention.

SCENE 1: WE ARE FAMILY!

Jewish family life has always been dramatic; the family is crucial to biblical narratives, rabbinic literature rules significantly on family relationships and the concept of *mishpacha* (close and not so close relatives and friends) remains a powerful idea. So it's not at all surprising that so many plays of 'Jewish interest' have been about families, from the family dramas of Yiddish theatre and Israel Zangwill's *The Melting Pot* (1908, revived 1938 and in 2017 at the Finborough Theatre), through to Clifford Odets' *Awake and Sing* (1935, revival at the Almeida in 2007), which explores the eternal family conflict of parents trying to control their children while the children try to lead their own lives.

Arnold Wesker's *Chicken Soup with Barley* (1956) is a seminal example of a UK Jewish family play, the first in a trilogy with *Roots* and *I'm Talking about Jerusalem*. The action spans twenty years of the lives of the immigrant Kahn family between 1936 and 1956, during which the shattering of their communist convictions parallels the disintegration of the family. A major revival at the Royal Court in 2011, starring Samantha Spiro as the matriarch Sarah Kahn whose ideals somehow outlive the blows dealt by domestic and global events, was a reminder that being overtly Jewish still had plenty to say in the late 1950s.

But one very particular cultural change that has accelerated over the past twenty years, noted by former *Boston Globe* theatre critic Ed Siegel, is that contemporary plays with explicitly Jewish content are different from those of earlier times because newer writers 'are all fascinated by what it means to be a Jew in the 21st century'. He makes the point that there's 'nothing overtly Jewish about Arthur Miller's most famous families, the Lomans in *Death of a Salesman* and the Kellers in *All My Sons*. David Mamet's desperate characters in his early plays *American Buffalo* and *Glengarry Glen Ross* could be anything.' Theatregoers mostly do not know or care whether Harold Pinter or Tom Stoppard are Jewish or 'Jew-ish'. And we, the audiences, value our freedom to bring our unique perspective – Jewish or not – to bear on revivals and give free rein to our own understanding of what we think is being represented.

Jewish playwrights over the last quarter of a century certainly have had the luxury of exploring our cultural concerns and just how we Jews fit into our societies. As Siegel observes, whereas older authors (Pinter, Bernard Kops, Wesker, Miller, Steven Berkoff) were concerned with less ethnically defined explorations of being Jewish within a society emerging after the Second World War, the concerns of current practitioners include the religious and the secular, modern families, being 'Jew-ish', power and influence, Israel and the diaspora. Siegel cites the American director Melia Bensussen, as noting a trope of 'negotiating the rift between a marginalized past but a theoretically assimilated present'. Contemporary authors are happier than previous generations to wash dirty linen in public and explore matters that may well be embarrassing and well beyond traditional Jewish stereotypes, though still through the medium of the modern family.

Berkoff's play *Sit and Shiver*, which had its European premiere at London's sadly missed New End Theatre, after a Los Angeles debut in 2004, sits right on the fault line between the eras. He uses this solecism of sitting *shivah* (the Jewish seven-day mourning period, where bereaved families are seated together for prayers and condolence visits at home) as a way of bringing out the clash between London's old East End, Yiddish-inflected culture and that of the new world inhabited by the next generation. The conflicting tensions are exacerbated when a visitor shows up bearing strange news that threatens to tear the family apart. By shifting the performance to a non-naturalistic style with his trademark physicality and choreography, Berkoff offers a comedy of Jewish manners that fondly and satirically depicts Jewish social situations, revealing how we all may be forced to re-evaluate our views given the circumstances. As Pinter says in *Old Times*, 'The past is what you imagine you remember, convince yourself you remember, or pretend you remember.'

Compare this with Stephen Laughton's 2018 play *One Jewish Boy* (Old Red Lion, London/West End transfer, 2020, curtailed by Covid-19). Mixed-race Alex and Jewish Jesse make a compelling lens through which to examine the dissonant realities of modern life. Laughton mixes the issue of an increase in antisemitic hate crime with the inevitable dilemmas and compromises of a modern mixed faith and race relationship. The play lets the audience recognise their own prejudices about race, intermarriage and social conventions, sharpened for the Jewish audience by the way Jeremy Corbyn's Labour Party was failing to deal with antisemitism in its own ranks, even as the play was acclaimed by critics and audience alike.

A musical equivalent of *One Jewish Boy* is Jason Robert Brown's *The Last Five Years*, which premiered in Chicago in 2001 and was first seen in London at the off-West End Menier Chocolate Factory in 2006, with a revival in 2016 at the St James Theatre (also off-West End.) Another successful revival at the Southwark Playhouse opened in February 2020, before closing and reopening twice thanks to the pandemic and it was subsequently reimagined online. Young up-and-coming Jewish novelist Jamie falls in love with non-Jewish struggling actress Molly. Their story is told almost entirely through songs and the shtick is that her songs begin at the end of their marriage and move backwards in time, while his start at the beginning of their affair and move forward to the end of their marriage. They meet in the middle when he proposes. As ever, the audience is invited to see not just the simple story of a doomed relationship but to reflect on the capricious nature of modern life. Despite Jamie's delicious opening number 'Shiksa Goddess', in reviews of the 2020 production, only the *Jewish Chronicle* bothered to comment on the Jewish angle.

Josh Azouz's play *The Mikvah Project* was first performed at Hackney's Yard Theatre in 2015, crossing London for a revival in 2020 at Richmond's Orange Tree Theatre. It is set around the esoteric bathing ritual in the Orthodox Jewish community. The 17-year-old Eitan is friends with Avi, a married man of 35; they are 'postmodern orthodox Jews' who go to the same north London synagogue, where Avi is a chorister, and see themselves as heterosexual until they share a kiss in the *mikvah*. There is plenty of room for exploring issues of guilt and vulnerability, but ultimately the mood is life-affirming, even celebratory, and enhanced by the beautiful liturgical music sung by Avi. Jewish audiences clearly brought their own age, sexual orientation and denominational perspectives to bear in their estimation and appreciation of the play – and they did turn out to see it, ensuring full houses.

According to Siegel, the American playwright Tony Kushner is the guiding spirit behind the current trend in which playwrights explore ethics and ethnicity in challenging ways – while celebrating a good family argument. Kushner is the author of *Angels in America* (1991/93), which enjoyed revivals at The Menier Chocolate Factory in 2012 and The National Theatre in 2017. By then, the value of a metaphorical examination of AIDS and homosexuality in America in the 1980s lay more in its evocation of the period than its message.

Kushner also wrote the book and lyrics for the 2003 musical *Caroline, or Change*, which was revived at Chichester Festival Theatre in 2017 with a West End transfer in 2019. This piece, loosely based on Kushner's childhood, resonated more immediately with Jewish audiences. It tells the story of a black woman who works as a maid for a Jewish family in 1963 Louisiana. As part of her work in the family's house, she is allowed to keep the pocket change she finds while doing laundry. But the coins are not there by accident: the family's young son, who has become close to Caroline and loves to spend time with her as she works, is surreptitiously leaving them for her in his pockets. This becomes a point of pride and even crisis for the maid, who cannot cope with changes in her own life and the growing civil rights movement. Caroline's dull domestic routine is enlivened by her fantasies: she conjures up a singing radio, washing machine, dryer and even the moon, all brought to life by the actors/singers portraying them, with a score that is a wonderful mix of spirituals, blues, Motown and klezmer. Kushner's vivid evocation of Jewish family life in the deep South, and the tensions with the more self-avowedly liberal New York grandparents visiting for Chanukah, chimed with all audiences. Though some critics and audience did not fully appreciate the show's magic realism, Kushner's invitation to all of us to keep questioning the extent of our own spiritual change seems as relevant now as it was in 1963.

Another American playwright, Joshua Harmon, also deals with that combination of entitlement and guilt that snares the contemporary Jewish condition in his 2018 play *Admissions* (UK premier Trafalgar Studios, 2019). *Admissions* follows the white neo-liberal headmaster of an American boarding school and his Jewish wife, who is also head of admissions. Their clever son Charlie fails to get into Yale, while his best friend, who is biracial, is admitted. Charlie's seventeen-minute rant about what he sees as the injustice of the situation prompted one critic to observe that, just like Donald Trump, Charlie is merely saying what everyone is thinking. The disconcerting comedy forces us to confront the uncomfortable truth: that we are all hypocrites when push comes to shove and it certainly reminds us that we are all potentially and as likely as not 'bad' people.

Harmon's scurrilously funny *Bad Jews* (USA 2012; UK 2014, Bath; 2015, London) explores what it means to be human within the confines of the Jewish-American family dynamic. As Harmon has commented in *Playbill*, 'This is a private fight within the family, and you're somehow intruding, which is an exciting, dangerous place for an audience to be.' After a beloved grandfather dies in New York, leaving a treasured piece of religious jewellery he succeeded in hiding from the Nazis, cousins fight not only over the family heirloom, but also about their faith, degree of cultural assimilation, lifestyle and partner choices. As with Berkoff's *Sitting Shiva*, we cringe at the stereotypes of (New Yorker) Jewishness but Harmon has them so extreme and the humour so vitriolic that audiences gasped as they roared with laughter.

The personal and the political is also a recurring trope in Jewish theatre over the past twenty years (as it was in the twenty years before that). Mike Leigh's

Two Thousand Years (2005) traverses the lives of three generations in a contemporary Jewish middle-class family, exploring politics, religion, identity and the hard questions posed by Israel and its relationships with its citizens and neighbours. Leigh links the issues of everyday Jewish family life to the big issues of the day through the crisis faced by the left-leaning, middle-class, secular Jewish couple at the heart of his story when their son becomes *frum* (religious). Much of the interest in the UK, at least, was generated because this was Leigh's first devised stage play for over a decade. In an interview for the *Guardian* about the play, Leigh said, 'While I walked away from a Jewish existence, lots of things carried on in my life: gastronomic obsession, massive amounts of reading Isaac Bashevis Singer and Saul Bellow. So one doesn't stop being Jewish.' Despite some curious plotting, Leigh shows us the shifting religious affiliation within one family as a metaphor for more universal truths, including the politics of identity and religion – even if sometimes we do not want to see them.

From the perspective of my role as arts editor for *JR*, I do admire the respect and care non-Jewish actors bring to their Jewish characters. In some ways, the lived experience of Jewish actors can overwhelm their role in a way that more considered, less mannered performances from non-Jewish actors do not. So it was remarkable to see the row that erupted over the musical *Falsettos* (book by William Finn and James Lapine, music and lyrics by Finn), which follows a dysfunctional family coming to terms with the AIDS crisis. It came to London's The Other Palace in 2019 after a successful Broadway revival in 2016. But the production was met with an astonishing outcry from Jewish theatrical royalty because, 'to the best of our knowledge, no one in the cast of the UK premiere is Jewish, and neither is the director or anyone on the team' – a point they made in an open letter to *The Stage*. How much this mattered seems to have depended on your willingness to have non-Jews playing Jews alongside your willingness to see non-gays playing some of the gay parts. It is indeed a very 'Jewish' show, with smatterings of Hebrew, Yiddish and references to gefilte fish and Jews being poor at sport. But like it or loathe it, in the end, like Kushner's *Angels*, it felt a curiously period piece that worked more in its evocation of the period than its message.

Pinter's 1964 *The Homecoming*, revived in London in 2008 (Almeida Theatre, Islington) and 2015 (Trafalgar Studios, West End), may have been better received in its revivals than in the original production, which was seen by many at the time as baffling and enigmatic. *The Homecoming* explores issues of sex, power and gender which arise when a philosophy professor visits his (Jewish) family after a nine-year absence and introduces his wife to his father, uncle and two brothers. Every family member is on the take; using and abusing each other is second nature and the language is shocking and brutal – but this is the way this family communicates. By 2008, audiences seemed to have much greater acculturated understanding and be more accepting of a tough plot line about the changing nature of marriage, marrying out and family life generally. Audiences had a unique opportunity in 2018–19 to ponder on the Jewishness or not of Pinter's plays thanks to producer/director Jamie Lloyd, who gave London audiences the chance to evaluate a considerable swathe of the playwright's work in his ambitious six-month retrospective 'Pinter at the Pinter' (Harold Pinter Theatre, 2018–19).

Patrick Marber's *Howard Katz* (2001, National Theatre) was another tilt at the portrayal of a secular Jew negotiating his way in an increasingly atheistic, if not godless, society. Despite his loss of faith, Katz still argues with God – as well as everyone else. The tragi-comic near-stereotypes rather galled at the time and it was hard to find much understanding of and empathy for Katz, despite an outstanding performance by Ron Cook. But this play about a hard-nosed and successful Jewish showbiz agent dealing with a mid-life crisis might just be worth a revival, unlike David Mamet's 2019 play *Bitter Wheat* (Garrick, London) centring around a depraved Hollywood mogul. Unusually for one of his works, this was a play that lost both its way and the critics, despite the draw of John Malkovich in a fat suit 'being' Harvey Weinstein.

Yet another play that uses the Jewish family as the prism through which to refract family secrets, religion and politics is Ryan Craig's 2011 work *The Holy Rosenbergs* (National Theatre). Interestingly, the play, about the impact of an international conflict on a single family living in Edgware, was attacked for being both anti-Palestinian and antisemitic – quite an achievement. David Rosenberg, whose life and business are both disintegrating, is trying to deal with the funeral of his son who has been killed fighting with the IDF in Gaza, while his lawyer daughter is working on a UN report into suspected IDF war crimes. Events rapidly compound into a mess of conflicting emotions and viewpoints. As ever, the quietly natural performance by Henry Goodman as the falsely jolly Rosenberg paterfamilias anchored the increasingly unrealistic unfolding of events. Like Miller, Craig tries to fuse the past, present, and future into competing versions of history, while showing how the seemingly domestic events of a Jewish family in a London suburb can encourage us to reflect on the challenges of global politics.

Craig's 2017 play *Filthy Business* (Hampstead Theatre) is powered by Sara Kestelman's Yetta, doing whatever is needed to keep the business in the family and the family in the business. This time Craig uses the Jewish family to look at social change through the device of the immigrant entrepreneur. For Yetta, the business is essentially an extension of herself and her worry about the kind of monument she might leave behind to children who do not seem to care as much as she does. The action of the play centres on the family's ensuing psychological conflicts over the years and, while they feel a little predictable and some of the characters verge on the stereotypical, the issue of the moral 'obligations' of Jewish business remains pertinent. This subject is also explored in Peter Flannery's play *Singer* (RSC 1989, Antony Sher and 2004, Oxford Stage Company, Ron Cook). Flannery shows us slum landlord Singer as he moves from surviving at whatever cost in Auschwitz to an England that is hardly welcoming to immigrants, especially those from the Caribbean. The play depicts stereotypes of Thatcherite capitalists and barely allows for nuances, but, sadly, it is based on some real Jewish characters of the time.

Even the family drama of others provides good material for the Jewish family. *Three Sisters on Hope Street* (Liverpool Everyman, 2008) by Diane Samuels and Tracy-Ann Oberman resets Chekhov's *Three Sisters* in the Jewish community of wartime Liverpool. As with Chekhov, the drama portrays young women filled with a sense of anomie trying to make sense of life in their fast-changing world. The parallels are hard to sustain but the production certainly makes the point of the universal in family plays. This process can be seen in reverse in the recent recasting of the Loman family in Miller's *Death of a Salesman* (Young Vic and Piccadilly Theatre, 2019) as a black family. All their yearning for the prosperity and success expected from hard work is dashed by casual but real prejudice. The social interactions here are heightened by the resetting and make for a timely reconsideration of the Willy Lomans of the world.

Another high-profile regional production that remained true to its northern roots in a city that is home to a large Jewish community is also a family story. When Simon Bent adapted *The Mighty Walzer*, Howard Jacobson's best-selling autobiographical novel, for the stage in 2016, the production's obvious home was Manchester's Royal Exchange Theatre. Manchester is Jacobson's native city and the setting for his comic tale of table tennis and teenage angst in a warm but dysfunctional Jewish family. Director Jonathan Humphreys gathered a terrific roll call of Jewish acting talent to evoke 1950s Jewish Manchester, with Elliot Levey as Jacobson's alter ego the eponymous Oliver Walzer, recalling his youth heading up a ping pong posse of nerdy teenagers and negotiating between the marital double act of his larger-than-life father Joel (Jonathan Tafler) and warm, worried mother Sadie (Tracy-Ann Oberman). Critics, theatregoers and Jacobson fans headed to Manchester to join local audiences in acclaiming a superb production, with imaginative associated events including an exhibition and walking tour.

There are, of course, dramas that fall outside the obvious categories but still have much to contribute to Jewish theatre and how it has changed. One beautiful and imaginative piece of immersive theatre tells the love story of artist Marc

Chagall and his wife Bella. Daniel Jamieson's *Flying Lovers of Vitebsk*, directed by Kneehigh Theatre's Emma Rice, featured two extraordinarily multi-talented performers in Marc Antolin and Audrey Brisson as the Chagalls, supported by a pair of equally talented musicians, production composer Ian Ross and fellow instrumentalist James Gow. It opened in Bristol in 2016 and triumphantly toured the UK, thrilling audiences and critics with its heady combination of dialogue, music, dance, circus skills and scenic design. It is a fitting evocation of the romance of the Chagalls,ß yet it does not shirk from providing a darker reality check on how the couple were caught up in the world-changing events of the First World War and the Russian Revolution and survived the antisemitism and pogroms that swept across Eastern Europe.

SCENE 2: THE HOLOCAUST

The view of the Holocaust from a seat in the theatre over the past twenty years has undergone significant change. There are no longer shocking discoveries to be experienced as the events are, fortunately, now well known and explored. The Holocaust stands apart from other historical events in that it is a National Curriculum requirement taught as part of the secondary-school history curriculum in the UK. First-hand survivor accounts, untold for fifty years, are necessarily more direct than plays, especially since reluctance to speak out and remember publicly was such a common survivor response to their experiences. Indeed, the UK's first official Holocaust Memorial Day only took place in 2001, perhaps a significant turning point for the exploration in drama of the genocide's continuing, often devastating effects.

Some of the best-known plays exploring those effects, such as Miller's *Broken Glass* or Diane Samuel's *Kindertransport*, take a more elliptical approach to the topic as a way of elucidation, recognising that nothing can compete with survivor testimonies or footage. Miller's 1994 play *Broken Glass* (revived London 2010, Tricycle Theatre, Kilburn, Watford Palace Theatre, 2018) is set in November 1938 and tells the story of the Gellburgs, a Jewish couple living in Brooklyn. Sylvia Gellburg suddenly becomes partially paralysed after reading about the events of Kristallnacht in the newspaper. Miller asks us to consider whether something badly broken can ever be repaired, be it a marriage, an identity or a country. On the showing of the 2018 revival, which resounded so well, the play had found its time and contemporary audience.

Kindertransport by Diane Samuels depicts the agony of separating a child from her parents as a matter of survival and wrestles with the consequences of that choice, with the subsequent calamitous results. Premiered in 1993, *Kindertransport* continues to be much studied and regularly performed, especially in British schools. The immediacy of theatre helps students to explore the challenging questions about behaviour and morality raised by the history of the Holocaust.

In Charlotte Eilenberg's 2002 play *The Lucky Ones*, premiered at Hampstead Theatre, the eponymous protagonists are also Kindertransport children; two couples who jointly own a chocolate-box country cottage, which they now (in 1968) decide to sell. Despite being brothers- and sisters-in-law, each couple has a different attitude as to how far they feel assimilated or outsiders. When the potential buyer, Lisa, turns out also to be from Berlin, an extraordinary condition of sale is demanded at the last minute. Decades later, the couples' second-generation children talk with Lisa, confronting the legacy that their parents have left them, and we are left pondering the struggle between remembering and forgetting.

Tom Stoppard's *Leopoldstadt* (2020, West End), whose genesis came from Stoppard's 80-year-old mother finally talking about her experience during the war, is hugely admired and enjoyed for the way Stoppard reckons with the past and for the emotional tug at the end. Audiences delight in sharing Stoppard's discovery of his Jewish roots even though some were aware that there was nothing new to be seen here. We admire, however, the sweep of history, the individual characters and their journey in Stoppard's most autobiographical play.

Contemporary audiences have also been receptive to more direct accounts such as Antony Sher's *Primo* (2004, National Theatre and film 2005, directed by Richard Wilson), based on Primo Levi's classic account of his Auschwitz experiences, 'If This Is a Man'; and David Greig's 2001 play *Dr Korczak's Example*, set in the shadows of the Warsaw Ghetto in 1942. The play examines life in an orphanage where escapism is key to survival and where the children's sense of togetherness is their bulwark against the tide of hate coming their way. Korczak's influence led to the creation of the UN Convention on the Rights of the Child in 1989 and knowledge of this influences how one considers the play. Frequent revivals include a 2012 production by the young people's theatre company Unicorn, accompanied by a comprehensive teacher's resource pack and, most recently, a well-received Leeds Playhouse production opening in January 2020 to coincide with Holocaust Memorial Day.

Martin Sherman's constantly revived 1979 play *Bent*, about the persecution of homosexuals in Nazi Germany around the time of the Night of the Long Knives, speaks immediately to the Jewish experience, as does *I Wish to Die Singing – Voices from The Armenian Genocide*, a 2015 play commemorating the centenary of the first genocide of the twentieth century, perpetrated by the Ottoman Turkish government against the Armenians, a Christian minority in a Muslim state.

Some 1.5 million people died in the atrocity. Author Neil McPherson, in his role as artistic director of the Finborough Theatre, also brought us in 2017 Miller's *Incident at Vichy*, the first professional production of the play in fifty years. Miller depicts a group of men detained in Vichy France in 1942, held for 'racial' inspection by German military officers and Vichy French police. The play focuses on the subjects of human nature, guilt, fear, and complicity and examines how the Nazis were able to perpetrate the Holocaust with so little resistance. Miller said of *Incident at Vichy*, 'What is dark if not unknown is the relationship between those who side with justice and their implication in the evil they oppose. The good and the evil are not compartments but two elements of a transaction.'

★★★

C.P. Taylor's *Good* (1981), scheduled for a star-studded revival (delayed due to Covid-19) with David Tennant and Elliot Levy, also demonstrates how seemingly decent people could have their lives and motives drastically altered by Nazi ideology during Hitler's regime in the Second World War. Halder, the treacherous, alienated academic, is first entranced by the Nazi party and later entrapped by the seeming necessity of its horrors. We are invited to consider how man in all frailty, wants to do and be seen to be doing good and 'the dilemma between the unspeakable horror of the deeds and the undeniable ludicrousness of the man who perpetrated them', as Hannah Arendt put it in her original piece on the Eichmann trial for the *New Yorker*. Perhaps we now have a better perspective with which to understand, as Joseph Brodsky wrote in the *New York Review of Books* in 1984: 'What we regard as Evil is capable of a fairly ubiquitous presence if only because it tends to appear in the guise of good.'

Others have ventured into full musical theatre to explore the Holocaust, with varying success, especially given that audiences over the last twenty years have been inoculated with the absurdity and anarchy of the irrepressible number 'Springtime for Hitler: A Gay Romp with Adolf and Eva at Berchtesgaden' in Mel Brooks' *The Producers*.

One critically unsuccessful attempt at portraying the Holocaust in a musical was *Imagine This* (2007, New London Theatre), a musical set in the Warsaw Ghetto about a troupe of actors trying to stage a play about the siege of Masada to inspire hope and optimism within the Jewish community. It was not just that the music, plot and lyrics did not work well enough together – but the concept itself was simply all too embarrassing.

In 2014, to commemorate the 60th anniversary of the Red Cross inspection of Terezin, Philip Glassborow (not Jewish) was commissioned by director

Adam Forde to write a new music theatre piece, *Welcome to Terezin*, featuring some of the songs that had actually been created and performed in Terezin. The piece was written for Guildford's Yvonne Arnaud Youth Theatre, who captured the defiant spirit of hope and optimism that appealed to audiences and this memorable work captivated audiences in Guildford and on the Edinburgh Fringe.

The most recent play in the UK dealing with 'Life unworthy of life', a Nazi term for those who had no right to live, is a reconstructed version of *The Last Cyclist*, a satire written in 1944 by young Czech playwright Karel Švenk while imprisoned in Terezín. While many inmates saw the dress rehearsal, the play was never produced as the Council of Jewish Elders feared reprisals given the brutal, devastating satire directly pointed at the Nazis. Švenk was murdered in Auschwitz a year later and the play lost. It was reimagined and staged by Naomi Patz in America in 1999 and has enjoyed a number of successful US revivals since. It premiered in the UK in Newcastle in February 2020 in a gripping, immediate and involving production by Robert Hersey, as part of the Brundibàr Arts Festival. *The Last Cyclist* is a play within a play: inmates of the camp rehearse the story of a bunch of insane asylum detainees, with the audience cast as Terezin inmates watching the dress rehearsal. The title comes from a joke familiar to Jews in Mitteleuropa between the wars. Three people are discussing the political situation. The first exclaims: 'The Jews and the cyclists are responsible for all our misfortunes!' The second asks, 'Why the cyclists?' And the third, 'Why the Jews?' The play follows a group of inmates who have escaped from an insane asylum and taken over the world. Because these lunatics hate their bike-riding physician, they target all cyclists and anyone who sells biking gear or is related to cyclists or has cyclist ancestors going generations back, blaming them for every trouble afflicting society.

Unlike the lives of those who survived the camps or escaped the Nazis on the Kindertransport, the lives of those who fled central Europe just in time are rarely portrayed. *The Ballad of the Cosmo Café* was part of the UK-wide Insiders/Outsiders Festival celebrating the contribution of émigré artists to British culture. This original piece of theatre recreates the much-loved Cosmo Café on London's Finchley Road that was especially frequented by émigrés. It was created by a team led by director and visual artist Pamela Howard and writer Philip Glassborow and is based on selected memories and stories compiled by the Cosmo research group, while the Cosmo writers' group transformed the memories into lyrics. With its refrain, 'room, shared bath, no kitchen', the work is an ode to the exigencies of life in bedsitland off 'Finchleystrasse' and a timely reminder of the loss and nostalgia felt by so many modern immigrants.

SCENE 3: THE ISRAEL QUESTION

As I argue from the start, it is the responsibility of audiences to interpret plays, recognising that theatre is nothing if not a space in which to engage in conversations and ideas and not somewhere to merely have your prejudices confirmed. For the gaze of Jewish audience members in particular, Israel brings a singular challenge – how to get increasingly comfortable feeling uncomfortable.

It would be wonderful to reflect on a swathe of plays by Israeli writers and theatre troupes performed in the UK over the last twenty years – but that has largely not been the case, either because producers feared insufficient audiences or because they feared having to face the chance of cultural boycotts. Plays about Israel are often about the rarely objective state of affairs between Israel and the Palestinians, in notable contrast to the plethora of Israeli television and films over the last ten years dealing with a range of domestic subjects, not always about the Middle East 'situation', the Holocaust or religion.

Consider first the *broiges* ('controversy' is not quite a translation that does the Yiddish justice) that flared up with *My Name Is Rachel Corrie*, a play based on the diaries and emails of activist Rachel Corrie, 23, killed in 2003 by an Israeli soldier operating a bulldozer in Gaza. The text was jointly edited by journalist Katharine Viner and actor Alan Rickman, who also directed it at the Royal Court in 2005. The critics were clear it was a work of left-wing agitprop with a hefty dose of unvarnished propaganda, with little effort to provide the context for the violence. The producers were also clear that the play made no pretence of being an objective or comprehensive analysis of the Israel/Gaza situation but merely reportage of a young American activist's enthusiasm about improving the world. It was revived at the Young Vic in 2017, complete with picketers waving Israeli flags and handing out counter-information leaflets claiming that Corrie was 'a young idealist manipulated by terrorist enablers'. But time and a certain degree of, one regrets to say, habituation to the 'situation' ('a plague on both your houses') make it somewhat easier to see the tragic personal story of a human being driven by what she saw as the best of motives.

Caryl Churchill wrote *Seven Jewish Children: A Play for Gaza*, a ten-minute work first staged in 2009 at London's Royal Court Theatre, in response to the 2008–9 Israeli incursion into Gaza. In seven scenes over seventy years, Jewish adults discuss what their children should be told about events in recent Jewish history. The play was widely condemned as antisemitic and anti-Israel, though Tony Kushner notably said that any play about the crisis in Gaza that did not arouse anger and distress probably missed the point. In response, Richard Stirling wrote *Seven Other Children*, 'the tragedy of the Palestinian child as a victim of a distorted education about Israel', to balance response to the debate, with Palestinian adults discussing what their children should be told about events in recent history. To paraphrase a comment from Stirling, the audiences at both plays were probably, regrettably, not there to have their minds stretched, but their prejudices confirmed.

Of course, Jews protesting about unfair portrayals on stage is nothing new. There was a riot at the opening night of Dibdin's *Family Quarrels* in 1802, with the crowd offended by Jewish stereotypes and the use of synagogue music. And then, as now, disapproval was expressed simply by staying away, notably from an 1818 production of Christopher Marlowe's *The Jew of Malta*.

Theatregoers also encountered *Via Dolorosa*, a monologue by David Hare at The Royal Court, London in 1998 and revived in 2002 in the West End, in which the playwright (who incidentally is married to Jewish fashion designer Nicole Farhi) shared his personal journey through the Israel-Palestine conflict and the extremist positions on both sides. In spring 2009, he followed this with two related first-hand accounts: *Berlin* (National Theatre), his very personal experience of the dichotomy between his perception of the German capital from history and literature and the reality of life there, and *Wall* (again at The Royal Court), reporting from both sides of the Israeli security barrier being erected in the West Bank. *The Guardian*'s Michael Billington dubbed him 'British Drama's leading foreign correspondent'. Hare was more opinionated this time but, more than ten years on, the Jewish audience, while by no means anti-Israel, was so much more inured to barbs about the long-running saga of the Israel/Palestine conflict. In 2019 *Wall* was reincarnated as an animated film by Cam Christiansen.

At the Edinburgh Fringe Festival in 2014, a group of fifty Scottish cultural figures called for the festival to boycott the Israeli production *The City* by Jerusalem-based company Incubator Theatre on the grounds that it was partially funded by Israel's Ministry of Culture. There were the usual arguments on both sides about freedom of artistic expression and the virtue signalling of a cultural boycott, including challenges from some Israel-based groups who support BDS.[1] In the end the company felt compelled to give up its venue at the Edinburgh Fringe, fuelling further squabbles about how far politics and arts should be answerable to each other.

---

1 The Boycott, Divestment, Sanctions (BDS) movement works to end international support for Israel's oppression of Palestinians and pressure Israel to comply with international law.

A rich variety of accounts of life on the ground in Israel/Palestine, from the point of view of Israelis and Palestinians themselves, sometimes contrasting, sometimes complementary – often in the same work – has also been presented on the British stage in the last twenty years.

Food can be relied on to bring people together – and divide opinions. *The Arab-Israeli Cookbook* is a piece of verbatim theatre[2] seen at the Gate Theatre in 2005, based on interviews in 2003 with people living in Israel and on the West Bank. The owner of a falafel shop shares his recipe while talking about the bomb attack on his shop. A woman tells how, after she was caught in a bomb blast, she went back to the targeted supermarket to get her shopping. A café owner divulges his secret recipe for hummus that few can eat as they cannot get to his village; a mother makes the Jewish new year meal for her family. The stories were equitably distributed between Jew and Arab, though different viewpoints saw bias everywhere, but it was yet another chance to understand just how communities in Israel live cheek by jowl and what it is like for ordinary people on both sides. Similarly, the extended Israeli Jewish family in Julia Pascal's 2015 play *Crossing Jerusalem* is attempting to cross the city to get to their favourite Arab eatery, now almost out of bounds after the second intifada. Pascal takes pains to research the lives of Arab Israelis and the restaurant owners share centre stage. During a run in Miami, Pascal received flak from Jewish press perceiving the play as anti-Israel, though the British press and audiences had no such problem during its run at London's Park Theatre.

Another piece of verbatim theatre designed to let voices from both sides speak was *Semites* (2018, London and Bristol), realised and staged with the support of Salaam Shalom, the Bristol-based Muslim/Jewish dialogue organisation focused on arts, media and education. The group aims to 'stimulate dialogue and understanding between Muslim and Jewish communities and the wider communities in which they live'. True to this remit, writer/performer Ben Nathan went to meet Palestinians and brought their words and those of Israelis to a UK audience, their verbatim testimonies showing just how differently both sides see events and each other. British-Jewish Nathan shared the stage with British–Jordanian actor Lara Sawalha to explore contrasting views of events and challenge the audience to confront historical facts and narratives while considering the legitimacy of both sides.

A glimmer of hope and recognition of failed opportunities came in 2017 with *Oslo*, the Tony Award-winning play by Jewish American playwright J.T. Rogers. The play is a dramatisation of the secret back-channel negotiations that took place

2   A form of documentary theatre made from the words of real people.

between Israel and the PLO prior to the Oslo Peace Accords of the 1990s. It enjoyed a sell-out run at the National Theatre and in its West End transfer. The plot follows the true story of the efforts of two Norwegian diplomats to bang political heads together by removing implacable enemies from their normal negotiating contexts and provide with them a retreat where they can get to know one another as individuals. The resulting Oslo Declaration of Principles was not a peace treaty but more a framework to facilitate further negotiations for a final agreement, and the play forced us to gaze longingly and hard at what might have been.

Under the Skin by Yonatan Calderon (performed at the Red Lion Theatre in 2018) is one of those rare plays performed in the UK that has been written by a contemporary Israeli. It is set in Tel Aviv during the 1991 Gulf War, and, through flashbacks to Nazi Germany in 1944, it tells the story of the love affair between a lesbian Nazi officer and one of her female Jewish prisoners in a concentration camp. The play is based on survivor testimonies and I found it to be a piece of shocking beauty, a telling account of how the way we view the past continues to shape us today.

Similar themes are grappled with in Tik-Sho-Ret Theatre Company's production of *5 Kilo Sugar* (Etcetera Theatre Camden, 2015).[3] The play follows Gur, whose late grandfather appears to him through the bodies of a variety of unsuspecting hosts in order to embolden him to right what his grandfather perceives as a historical wrong perpetrated during the 1940s in post-war Eastern Europe. Tik-Sho-Ret Theatre aims to give a platform to Israeli and Jewish theatre in the UK, to encourage collaborations through cultural and artistic exchange and to promote communication and co-existence – and the production ran without problem at the Edinburgh Festival that year.

Another engaging and perceptive contribution to our understanding of life in Israel was the 2016 play *Knock Knock* (Etcetera Theatre). Niv Petel played one character throughout the whole play, the mother of a young army conscript. The mother's job is to tell bereaved parents the worst, to make that dreaded knock on the door, and to work with them through the grief and loss that will form part of the rest of their lives. But when the time comes for her own son to join the army, she faces a life-changing dilemma.

Mike Kember's *Not Quite Jerusalem*, revived at the Finborough in 2020, harks back to a more hopeful period in 1979, when Egypt signed a peace treaty with Israel. Four non-Jewish 20-something Brits – Mike, Carrie, Pete and Dave – ditch England to be guest workers on an Israeli kibbutz. The play is much more about Brits abroad and what they learn about themselves than any exploration

3 Tik-Sho-Ret stands for 'communication' in Hebrew.

of kibbutz life and kibbutzniks. Jewish audience members must have been glad to revel in the stock kibbutz characters without the need for any sense of guilt or worry about Arab-Israeli issues.

But even Shakespeare was not immune to the politics of the Middle East. Israel's Habima theatre company was invited as part of the Cultural Olympiad accompanying the London 2012 Olympics to perform *The Merchant of Venice* in Hebrew. This was part of a programme to stage some seventy productions related to Shakespeare's plays, over half of which were in a language other than English. Pro-Palestinian activists disrupted the show by unfurling Palestinian flags and shouting comments throughout. There were also small-scale demonstrations by pro-Palestinian and pro-Israeli groups outside the venue. The performance carried on despite the disruptions, with Globe Artistic Director Dominic Dromgoole advising the audience beforehand; 'If there are disturbances, let's be perfectly calm. Don't get angry. You're not watching politicians or policymakers. You are watching artists who are here to tell a story.' How this story of Shylock has been told by other companies over the last twenty years is the meat of the next section.

SCENE 4: SHYLOCK TAKES TO THE TWENTY-FIRST-CENTURY STAGE

In 2016, *Romeo and Juliet* topped a YouGov poll commissioned to celebrate the 400th anniversary of Shakespeare's death, ranking his plays in order of how many respondents had seen them. *The Merchant of Venice* came fifth and I suspect most audiences consider Shylock to be central to the action – some perhaps even mistaking him for the eponymous Merchant himself. Indeed, actor Elliot Levey, self-confessed 'go-to Jew' on stage, screen and airwaves, vowed in a recent interview with me that he would not play Shylock in any production where the director placed 'the Jew' centre-stage.

'The Jewish wrestling with Shylock is (therefore) always reflective on a specific time and place,' says Edna Nashon in the introduction to 'Jewish Responses to *The Merchant of Venice*'. *The Merchant of Venice* is inherently antisemitic but also instructive about prejudice, greed, mercy and family, and it is rarely played nowadays without nuance and more than a passing nod to contemporary antisemitism or the Holocaust. So, looking at treatments of Shylock in performance is one more way to get a feel for the changing scope and nature of the Jewish theatrical landscape over the past twenty years.

Twenty years ago, Henry Goodman won the Olivier Award for Best Actor and Trevor Nunn Best Director for a production of *The Merchant*. Inevitably the focus was on Goodman's very human portrayal of Shylock plus a reflection on what his lived-through Jewish experience brought to the part. His heart-breaking reaction on hearing from his fellow Jew Tubal that his fugitive daughter Jessica had exchanged a ring she had taken from him for a pet monkey touched audiences, especially when he reached for a framed photograph of his long-dead wife Leah with the words, 'Thou torturest me, Tubal. It was my turquoise. I had it of Leah when I was a bachelor. I would not have given it for a wilderness of monkeys.' What Nunn brought to the early 1930s central European setting of the production, so prefiguring the Holocaust, was action not in the text, notably Tubal leaving the court appalled at Shylock's intransigence and Shylock, when finally forced to take off his kippah (skullcap), putting it in the balance he brought to weigh his pound of flesh. Shylock finally became a true human being and not a cypher.

A similar focus on what the lived experience of the actor brings to the role was exemplified in a 2015 production at the RSC starring award-winning Palestinian-Israeli actor Makram J. Khoury. Audiences inevitably wondered about the parallels of his experience as a man caught between two worlds in his native country. Certainly, when Christian Venice shows its contempt by spitting on Shylock's 'Jewish gabardine', the gasp of horror that ran through the audience was even more of a shock wave than the similar audience reaction when this treatment was meted out to Jonathan Pryce's dignified Shylock in the 2015 production at the Globe. This latter production casts the Venetians as hard-hearted devils and Shylock leaves the stage after a Catholic conversion mouthing the word 'credo'. Once more, we have all become increasingly comfortable feeling uncomfortable when watching *The Merchant*, helped by actors and directors positively wanting to downplay the institutionalised antisemitic stereotype, which was written at a time when few people in Shakespeare's England would ever have met a practising Jew.

A production directed by Rupert Goold (RSC, 2011, with Patrick Stewart as Shylock and Almeida, 2014, with Ian McDiarmid in the role) transposes the action to Las Vegas, with Shylock the casino-owning venture capitalist and the casket scene now a games how, complete with live transmission screens. This Shylock has adapted to the common cultural values around him, something increasingly secular audiences could readily identify with, and it was poignant when this assimilated Jew, used to negotiating his way in an antisemitic world, is forced to be 'Jewish' – and then Christian, forcing us to recognise that assimilation depends on the receptiveness of the host society.

Playwright Julia Pascal refracts the legacy of the Holocaust through the lens of *The Merchant* in *The Shylock Play* (Arcola, 2007), its protagonist a Warsaw Ghetto survivor who visits the Venice Ghetto to find a theatre company about to play *The Merchant of Venice* right there. Pascal asks us to confront the prospect that the text set the seeds for contemporary antisemitism. And she also prefigured a theatrical first – the staging of *The Merchant* in the Venice Ghetto – that actually happened only in 2016 to mark the 500th anniversary of the Venetian ghetto's founding.

The various themes of the play are also used as teaching aids in schools and the fact that Shylock in the RSC's 2019 *First Encounters with Shakespeare: The Merchant of Venice* was both female and Israeli seemed to matter not one jot to the 7–13 year-olds for whom it was created. Shani Erez's fine Shylock made perfect sense as an embattled lone Jewish businesswoman and conflicted mother of a rebellious daughter. The whole cast under Robin Belfield's direction refused to shirk the discomfiting elements of the play and the fine balance between comedy and tragedy, even for such a young audience, made this first encounter with the Bard one I am confident they will recall for years to come.

It is crystal clear why the uneasy status quo between Christian and Jew is irrevocably ruptured by Jessica's betrayal of family and community and why her elopement tips Shylock into a single-minded quest for bloody revenge. The children I interviewed afterwards were comfortable talking about hard moral choices.

At the time of writing, Tracy-Ann Oberman is set to be the next woman to play Shylock in a new production of the play set in the East End of the 1930s, with Shylock as the mother figure running her business having fled the pogroms in Russia, and the Venetians recast here as supporters of the British Union of Fascists. With Shylock as a single mother, I expect Oberman's take to demonstrate just how far we have come in trying to reclaim the character.

But, writing in the *Guardian*, Howard Jacobson reminds us that in the end, '*The Merchant of Venice* is a play not a treatise, and that we would not expect Shylock to be sentimentalised. He does not become, by virtue of what we have learned, a man forgiven and explained.' We do not always have to see Shylock as a 'post-Holocaust improvement on the original'. Our time and tide give this generation the opportunity and freedom to perceive *The Merchant of Venice* as less problematic than it was more than twenty years ago. As Aviva Dautch, *JR*'s executive director, cogently argues in an article for the British Library, these modern, nuanced explorations of *The Merchant of Venice* force us to recognise the contradictions in ourselves, 'speaking about principles we don't always observe ourselves, loving those close to us while mistreating others, at times victim at times perpetrator and, in our complexity, fully human'.

SCENE 5: WHERE NEXT?

To sum up, a canter through Jewish theatre over the last twenty years, at least from the perspective of the audience or theatre critic, reveals just how far Jews, along with many elements of society, have embraced Jewish uniqueness and are prepared to celebrate it. We have understood how our acculturated understanding means we do not have to be the same as others to feel confident we belong within our communities. This has allowed writers, directors and us the audience to feel more assertive and self-assured in examining the intersection between the common cultural values around us (including antizionism and antisemitism) and the realities of the various aspects of Jewish life today. We are increasingly at ease being annoyed by what we see, recognising that theatre is nothing if not a space in which to engage in conversations and ideas and not merely to have your prejudices confirmed.

Live theatre allows us to experience situations that we may never personally encounter and in a way that is unique for that never-to-be-repeated performance. Theatre holds up a mirror to our own experiences that permits us to reflect on our own lives in a more immediate way than through other media. So, what might we expect in the next twenty years for both theatre practitioners and audience members?

Of course, there will be the revivals and re-interpretations of a range of plays to make us re-evaluate our attitudes at the time we first saw them and just how far our perceptions have come in their acculturated appreciation. Wesker's *I'm Talking About Jerusalem*, in which a couple moves from London to a desolate part of Norfolk where they intend to build the new Jerusalem, might currently seem very apposite, now that the Covid-19 pandemic has triggered a reappraisal of urban living, with many leaving cities for greener pastures.

A good exemplar is Arthur Schnitzler's 1912 *Professor Bernhardi*, superbly updated by Robert Icke as *The Doctor*, with an outstanding performance by Juliet Stevenson in the title role (Almeida, 2019, scheduled for West End post-pandemic). The original, played in its Viennese setting in a revival at the Arcola in 2005, explores Viennese antisemitism where a Jewish doctor is castigated for not giving a Catholic priest permission to administer the last rites to a patient. In Icke's version, Dr Ruth Wolff is a secular Jew in charge of a hospital, who stops the priest from seeing a 14-year-old girl dying after a self-induced abortion. The incident goes viral and threatens Ruth and the hospital. Icke takes the opportunity to expand the moral questions to race, gender and class, amplifying the discord by having white actors and women play black characters and men – and vice-versa. From the viewpoint of 'Jewish' theatre, *The Doctor* shows us the perils of steering your way through life only through the lens of your own tribe's shared experiences of perceived injustice; and the problems generated by an unreasonable refusal to even consider the principled views of others.

One of the most eagerly awaited productions cut short by the pandemic was the UK premiere at The Menier Chocolate Factory in London of *Indecent*, by the American playwright Paula Vogel. The play explores the origins of Yiddish writer Sholem Asch's controversial play, *The God of Vengeance*, where according to Asch's great-grandson, journalist and Yiddishist David Mazower, 'Sex, prostitution, lesbianism and the desecration of a Torah scroll grabbed the headlines.' That Tony Award-winning director Rebecca Taichman chose to bring the play to this small, but high-profile, theatre in a former Chocolate Factory is a testament to the space's reputation as a home for Jewish work under its founder and artistic director David Babani. Its productions include work by Tom Stoppard, Jack Rosenthal, Ryan Craig and Patrick Marber. It has also staged *Fiddler on the Roof* (2018) and work by Stephen Sondheim including *Assassins*, *Sunday in the Park with George*, *A Little Night Music* and *Merrily We Roll Along*; plus Leonard Bernstein's *Candide*. I expect to see more groundbreaking, well-received work at a theatre that certainly punches above its weight.

I expect to see even more plays using the Jewish family as the prism through which to diffract views of the world, for this looks like a continuing productive generative source. Expect themes relating family matters to climate change, human rights, corporate sustainability and religious and intra-religious conflicts. Not all of these will originate in North America – the UK has a fine tradition of Jewish playwrights and playwriting. We might finally have more plays from Israel in which the fact that the characters are Jewish or Israeli or Holocaust survivors will be largely incidental to the plot line.

Along with theatre practice in general, we are likely to see fewer 'well-made plays'[4] and possibly fewer plays of ideas. Stoppard himself has complained he has to dumb down his plays for modern audiences, not because they are lazy or stupid but because of the fracturing of cultural schemata in which we are now all so differently schooled.

But expect even more immersive experiences such as the 2008 Israeli theatre piece *Not By Bread Alone* from the 'Nalaga'at' Deaf-Blind Acting Ensemble, which had a UK run at London's Arts Depot in 2010. It featured eleven deaf-blind Jewish, Muslim and Christian Israeli actors kneading, raising and baking bread on stage as they told their stories. It proved an extraordinarily vivid, pow-

---

4 Summed up by Wilkie Collins as 'Make 'em laugh; make 'em weep; make 'em wait.'

erful and thought-provoking experience about the nature of communication – achieved in the time it took to bake bread.[5]

We will undoubtedly have access to more streamed or Zoomed plays too. The Covid-19 pandemic has proven that theatre can adjust to the digital age – perhaps we do not always need to travel to small, crowded spaces; we have seen how rehearsed readings and performances can be staged effectively online.

This should give space for productions that tackle more esoteric matters of initially limited appeal, such as arcane religious dispute or enigmatic moral choices. America, of course is already well ahead here; consider Phys Ed.'s *The Talmud*, 'a genre-bending performance that draws from a century of Chinese martial arts and a single chapter of The Talmud – a fifth-century text of Rabbinic Judaism'. It blends Kung-Fu movie cinematography and choreographed Talmudic debate, exploring how ancient traditions endure across generations.

And there will undoubtedly be more shows bridging the gap between theatre and gaming, with physical or virtual corridors to choose to explore. At the 2019 JCC Maccabi Games (an Olympic-style event welcoming thousands of Jewish teenagers from across the world), more than half of the athletes also signed up to play video games such as *The Shivah*, an adventure game in which players become a rabbi with struggling faith suspected of murdering a former congregant of the minister's synagogue; and *Vampire: The Masquerade — Redemption*, a role-playing game part set in the Jewish Quarter of medieval Prague. The Covid-19 pandemic has accelerated the readiness of 'silver surfers' to accept digital tools for the creation and sharing of content and it only takes the right word of mouth for shows to 'go viral'.

Regrettably, as David Herman noted in an article for *The Critic*, this all comes at a time when the golden age of theatre critics is passing. Journalists who know and care about theatre and who are more than merely entertaining and informative are in shorter supply. 'Who, then, will champion the new and the bold, in an increasingly conformist climate?' Let's hope that *JR* continues to provide those fresh perspectives on Jewish culture over the next twenty years and beyond and, to quote Howard Jacobson, continues to 'rescue English Jews from the curse of the parochial'.

5   The audience experience went further, for alongside the performance space, the company had installed the Blackout Restaurant, where visually impaired waiters accompanied their guests to a meal in total darkness – thus making the audience experience both immersive and empathetic.

APPENDIX 1: BIBLIOGRAPHY

Selected articles and books consulted:

Arendt, Hannah, *Eichmann in Jerusalem—I*, www.newyorker.com/magazine/1963/02/16/eichmann-in-jerusalem-i

Billington, Michael, *J is for Jewish Dramatists,* www.theguardian.com/stage/2012/feb/14/jewish-dramatists-modern-drama

Brodsky, Joseph, *A Commencement Address*, www.nybooks.com/articles/1984/08/16/a-commencement-address/

Dahlgreen, Will, *Shakespeare 400 years on: every play ranked by popularity*, yougov.co.uk/topics/lifestyle/articles-reports/2016/04/22/shakespeare-400

Grant, Linda, *Mike Leigh comes out*, www.theguardian.com/film/2006/apr/18/theatre.religion

Hetrick, Adam, *Roundabout Announces Second Extension of Joshua Harmon Comedy Bad Jews*, www.playbill.com/article/roundabout-announces-second-extension-of-joshua-harmon-comedy-bad-jews-com-210822#

Hoffman, Jordan, *UK writer wonders if good barriers truly make good neighbors in film, 'Wall'*, www.timesofisrael.com/uk-writer-wonders-if-good-barriers-truly-make-good-neighbors-in-film-the-wall/

Jacobson, Howard, *Villain or victim, Shakespeare's Shylock is a character to celebrate*, www.theguardian.com/books/2016/feb/05/villain-victim-shylock-shakespeare-howard-jacobson

Nahshon, E. and Shapiro, M. (eds) *Wrestling with Shylock – Jewish Responses to the Merchant of Venice* (Cambridge University Press, 2017)

Rosenberg, Harold, *Is There a Jewish Art?*, www.commentarymagazine.com/articles/harold-rosenberg-2/is-there-a-jewish-art/

Siegel, Ed, *Jewish-American Playwrights Are Grappling With Identity Head On*, www.wbur.org/artery/2020/01/02/jewish-american-playwrights-identity-assimilation

Steinberg, Rachel, *Artists accuse musical of 'Jewface' for not casting Jewish actors*, www.thejc.com/news/uk/artists-accuse-producers-of-jewface-for-casting-non-jewish-actors-in-open-letter-1.487641

FROM THE *JR* ARCHIVE

'SO WHAT IS JEWISH THEATRE?', BY DEBORAH FREEMAN

For JR's July 2007 issue, playwright Deborah Freeman gave her views on attending the International Festival of Jewish Theatre in Vienna, and grappled with the question of what 'Jewish Theatre' means, if anything at all.

Deborah Freeman is a playwright, short story writer and occasional poet. Her plays include Candlesticks, The Song of Deborah *and* Remedies. *Her short story collection,* Tell it Not, *will be published in January 2022 by Red Heifer Press, USA.*

An International Festival of Jewish Theatre, incorporating the World Congress of Jewish Theatre, took place in Vienna in March. Its umbrella title was: Tikun Olam (Repairing the World). Like all theatre practitioners, Jewish ones believe that through theatre the world can become a better place.

Day One: Warren Rosenzweig, of the Jewish Theatre of Austria, opens the proceedings. Warren was once an unaffiliated New York actor. Now his life's work is to promote the renaissance of Jewish theatre culture in Vienna.

Theodore Bikel, keynote speaker of the opening session, tells us Jewish Theatre is all or any of: 'high art, low art, naturalism, stylisation, political and apolitical'. I think: OK, that covers everything. I look forward to the next few days. Musing on the question as to whether creating something Jewish might 'set us apart', he adds: 'From the particular one reaches the universal. One flower in a big field. The Jewish flower.'

Dinner, the first night. Austrian actress Inge Maux sings Yiddish songs. Inge was born in 1944 to a mother who had successfully concealed her Jewish identity. But when school friends insisted she looked Jewish, Inge asked her mother why this should be. Her mother revealed the truth, and teenager Inge began to investigate her roots.

After dinner: a rehearsed reading of Warren's play *Der Judenstaat*. About Theodore Herzl – himself a Viennese playwright (though better-known as a liberal journalist). This reading takes place in the chill, darkly echoing neogothic Votivkirche. An unlikely setting for a play about the forces that led the Jewish people to their new land of blue skies.

Day Two: Atay Citron, Professor of Drama at Haifa University, talks about his years as Artistic Director of Israel's Alternative Theatre Festival. This festival takes place annually in Arab Jaffa. Jewish Israelis flock to it, to enjoy its cultural collaborations.

We watch videos of Arab and Hasidic fusion music, and the opening ceremony of last year's festival based on Sufi poetry and circle dancing. The conference finds the vision of a mystically spinning Israeli theatre both lively and soothing. Citron shows us Arabs and Jews seeking a common language through the medium of Indian movement theatre and pleases all of us.

Evening: Dinner and 'cabaret' at the Piaristenkeller, a restaurant as old as Imperial Vienna, with a hat museum and a wine cellar beneath us, in a maze of underground corridors lined with old wood barrels, the air thick with rich bouquets of wine and Habsburg legends.

Under us lies the history of Imperial Vienna. On the tiny stage sits Ruth Schneider, daughter of the Viennese Yiddish actress Klara Meisels and the playwright and chief dramaturge of the Jüdische Künstlerspiele in the Nestroyhof Theatre, Abisch Meisels. Ruth Schneider left Austria for London in 1938. Now she is here again, with her grandson, writer/comedian David Schneider. Also with them is Sanford Goldfless, son of Jacob Goldfliess, founder and director of the Jüdische Künstlerspiele in the Nestroyhof. In 1942, after eleven months internment in southern France, Goldfliess escaped to America.

Yiddish theatre in Austria in the 1920s and 30s was itself a culture of nostalgia. The Jews had come to Vienna from their Yiddish-speaking lives in the shtetl of Eastern Europe. And here we now are, another stratum of the mountain that is our cultural history.

Next: performances by Canadian Sharon Feder, Israeli Howard Rypp, and American Naava Piatka. But the Israeli has previously been Canadian, the Canadian has a family that came from Europe, and the American is of Lithuanian origin. Feder's piece is post-modern, surreal, Piatka's is in memory of her actress aunt in the Vilna Ghetto, and Howard Rypp has adapted *Gimpel the Fool* by Isaac Bashevis Singer, himself of Poland and then America. Moving and on the move, Jewish theatre is kaleidoscopic in form and full of emotion.

Warren Rosenzweig and Sanford Goldfless speak about a different venue. The Nestroyhof building, not far from here, survived the war only to become the store-room of a supermarket chain. Now, they say, is the time to work towards reclaiming it, opening it as an International Jewish Theatre.

Carolina, a Viennese gentile, studied Jewish culture at school and concluded that 'Jewish History is part of Austrian history'. Later she formed a group The Goyim – which performed klezmer pieces. Currently, she is setting to music Jewish poetry of 1920s Vienna. She declares: 'Jewish culture has a future. It must have a future.' She means in Austria. We mean in Austria too, as we applaud. Although the Israelis at my table ask bluntly: 'Why recreate anything Jewish here? Why don't they come to Israel?'

Day Three: Israeli playwright Motti Lerner lectures on political theatre, once again drawing a distinction between particularist and universalist themes. His conceptual framework is of 're-examination'. Of the very foundations of Judaism, no less – this, he says, being one of theatre's tasks.

A re-examination of the place of religion in Jewish and Israeli politics: of Israel-Arab relations; of the interface between Judaism and other religions; of pluralism (or not); of the responsibility of Jewish communities to other communities; of Jewish-Muslim conflicts; of antisemitism, Holocaust denial, Jewish historical memory; of Hebrew, Yiddish, Ladino; of the Jewish world and, of course, of globalisation. He misses out global warming.

Now theatre practitioners from Strasbourg, Sao Paulo, Melbourne, and Moscow, under the chairmanship of Atay Citron discuss the nature of Jewish theatre. I wish for an on-site anthropologist, who might identify in the people and their processes, where Jew ends and Russian, Australian, Brazilian, Frenchman, begins.

In the afternoon, Shimon Levy, Professor of Drama at Tel Aviv University presents 'The Bible as Theatre', with an accompanying performance by a stunning German actress in a red dress. We watch the biblical tale of Avigail and King David in an improvised dramatisation.

Later, at the International Playwrights' Forum, we hear extracts from eleven different Jewish plays in the evocative building of the Vienna Jewish Museum.

Day Four: Moti Sandak introduces his website: 'All about Jewish Theatre'. He has spent years setting up this database. The aim of 'All about Jewish Theatre' is: 'Recollect our past, understand our present and plan for the future.'

Over afternoon tea at the Australian ambassador's Residence, we watch a DVD about Australian Deborah Leiser-Moore's 'Jewish conceptual theatre practices'. She shows us physical theatre, visual, oral, surreal. The script, she insists, will only come about at the end of the process, if at all.

Finally I get it! The whole Jewish world is here, right inside our conference. Here are the Hasidim, the performance artists, who believe, like Leiser-Moore that dancing, singing and the moods of the heart create theatre. In opposition stand the Mitnagdim – the purists, who like a script made all of words. Like the old days when scholars required words on a page, until the Hasidim stood up to sing and dance their way to heaven.

Shabbat comes. Three visiting groups send representatives to the Friday night service. One group comprises returning children of the city. Another is at a Vienna university conference on the history of Austria's Jewish communities.

Final day: The last day of this kaleidoscopic conference – as varied as the others. Robin Hirsch of New York's Greenwich Village reads from memoirs of a post-war childhood in St John's Wood, London. In the afternoon, in an atelier in Vienna's Turkish quarter, American Yiddishist Murray Wolfe and New York Drama Professor/Holocaust survivor Saul Elkin both perform again. Both move me to tears.

Night, and the final piece of the jigsaw. American writer/actress Brenda Adelman performs *My Brooklyn Hamlet*. Adelman, half-sister to Warren Rosenzweig himself, tells the story of her childhood. This is the particular, the Hamlet story, becoming if not universalised, Judaised. Her father shot her (and incidentally Warren's) mother, then a few months later, married their aunt. This is theatre with the lid off, raw but disciplined. Passion, pain, truth and then love, all in an hour. The audience, me included, are drained.

After a closing performance of this intensity and brilliance, I no longer care whether my theatre is Jewish or not. Neither, I can assure you, will theatre repair our world. But I can promise you this: at its best – Jewish or otherwise – it reflects and illuminates it.

Incident at Vichy by Arthur Miller, at the Finborough Theatre, 2017. With (from left to right) Gethin Alderman, Edward Killingback, Jeremy Gagan and James Boyd. (Scott Rylander/ArenaPAL)

Welcome To Terezin by Philip Glassborow at Yvonne Arnaud Youth Theatre, Guildford, Surrey, 2014. With cast members of the Yvonne Arnaud Youth Theatre. (YAYT)

The Last Cyclist by Karel Švenk at Gosforth Civic Theatre, Newcastle, as part of the Brundibár Arts Festival, 2020. (Brundibár Arts Festival)

The Ballad of the Cosmo Café created by Pamela Howard with Philip Glassborow (writer), at St Peter's Church Hall, Belsize Square, London, 2019. With Grace Lovelass (left) and Valerie Minifie. (Kyle Nudo)

5 Kilo Sugar by Gur Koren at the Space on the Mile, Edinburgh, 2015. With Spencer Cowen (left), Tom Slatter and Michal Banai. (Tik-sho-ret. Photo: Shira Klasmer)

Knock Knock by Niv Petel at the Etcetera Theatre, London, 2016. With Niv Petel as Ilana/Elad. (Chris Gardner)

Not Quite Jerusalem by Paul Kember at the Finborough Theatre, 2020. With Russell Bentley and Miranda Braun. (Kirsten McTernan)

Not by Bread Alone by the Nalaga'at Deaf Blind Acting Ensemble at the Nalaga'at Centre, Tel Aviv, Israel, 2008. With members of the Nalaga'at cast. (Nalaga'at Centre)

The Family I Never Knew by Ardyn Halter, oil on canvas, 205 x 208cm, 1981. (Photo: Ardyn Halter)

House, House by Ruth Rix, oil on canvas, 92 x 72cm, 2016. (Photo: Hugh Rix)

Home Life, Looking On 1 by Susie Mendelsson, acrylic on paper, framed 70 x 90cm, 1999.
(Photo: Dick Makin)

Vacant Strandkorb (large) by Judith Tucker, oil on canvas, 152 x 121cm, 2006. (Photo: Judith Tucker)

Places to Remember II, detail by Lily Markiewicz, cibachrome on canvas 120 x 82cm, 1995 (Photo: Lily Markiewicz)

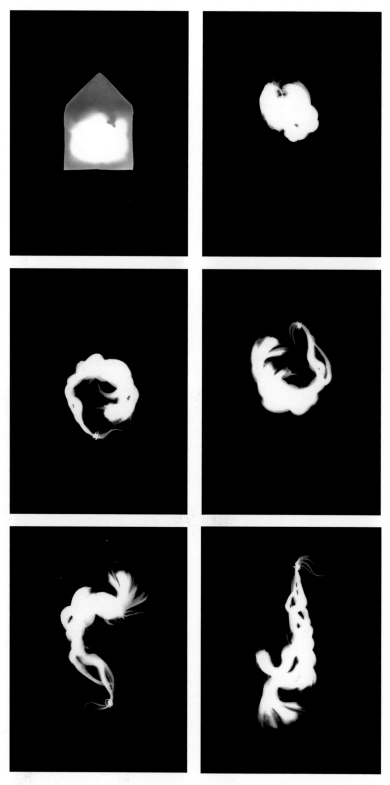

My Name Is Sara by Sara Davidmann, six hand-printed photograms on
resin-coated paper, each print 40.5 x 30.5cm, 2018. (Photographs courtesy
of the artist)

FROM THE *JR* ARCHIVE

'MY TEENAGE HERO', BY MIKE LEIGH

Director Mike Leigh was in his teens when the work of Arnold Wesker, who died in April 2016, blasted through the cultural scene of the 1950s. In this article from July 2016's issue of JR, *Leigh remembered the thrill of seeing a former East End Jewish boy take on the establishment and inspire a generation.*

Mike Leigh is a film and theatre director, screenwriter and playwright. He has been nominated for seven Academy Awards and in 1993 won the award for Best Director at Cannes for Naked. *He has also won the Palme d'Or for his 1996 film* Secrets & Lies, *as well as several BAFTAs.*

If you were a nice Jewish boy born in the 1940s, and you weren't called something Old Testament, like Michael, David or Jonathan, you'd be Anthony, Leslie, Geoffrey or even Barry. Half a generation earlier, the fashion had been the likes of Harold, Bernard or Arnold, of all of which there was an abundance.

So imagine how exciting it was, for the tiny handful of us who were concerned with such esoteric things as culture, to discover, in the late 1950s, that not one, but three young London East End Jewish working-class dramatists had burst onto the scene – a Harold, a Bernard and an Arnold.

In time, I would come to know all three writers personally, although none of them intimately. Of the trio, only Harold Pinter was actually an influence on my own work (the first play I ever directed was *The Caretaker* at RADA in 1962), and over the years he was always positive and supportive.

Bernard Kops' first volume of autobiography, *The World Is A Wedding*, is a splendid evocation of the Jewish East End in the 30s and 40s. As to my own dealings with him, nothing can be usefully reported here.

But back in 1959, although we were aware of Pinter and Kops, it was Arnold Wesker who most came to our attention, and with whom we immediately identified.

We were in the youth group Habonim. We were chaverim. We were budding socialists. We took part collectively in the CND Aldermaston March. We went hiking and camping, and we sang folk songs. Our parents despaired of us and called us 'schlochs' because we wore open-neck shirts and polo-neck pullovers and sandals, and the girls among us didn't wear make-up. And while our 'respectable' well-groomed contemporaries sat flirting in fashionable coffee bars, we debated serious issues like the bomb and capital punishment – and of course, the kibbutz, and whether to go on aliyah.

Then, suddenly, on the BBC TV *Brains Trust*, there was Arnold Wesker, ex-member of Habonim, wearing his polo-neck and his CND badge, and being cheeky in our own lingo to the likes of establishment figures Malcolm Muggeridge, Marghanita Laski and Alan Bullock.

What a hero he was. We sought out his plays, and read them avidly. At the great Habonim Camp in Brittany in the summer of 1959, we staged a performance of *Roots* in the marquee. A year later, en route for Israel aboard the SS *Artzah*, one of the rusting hulks that had run the gauntlet of the British only a few years earlier, crammed with survivors, we argued about the relative merits of *Chicken Soup with Barley* and *I'm Talking about Jerusalem*.

At one point, Arnold was invited to come and talk to us at a Habonim holiday seminar somewhere in Berkshire, but he cancelled at the last minute. Years later, when I recalled this to him, he was adamant that this couldn't have happened – he always honoured his commitments, and never let anyone down. This was true, of course: he was diligent in his unselfish attentiveness to all and sundry. (Plainly, something had detained him back in 1960, but he endearingly insisted that the story was implausible!)

The second time I didn't meet Arnold was in 1965. I was the assistant director at the new Midlands Arts Centre in Birmingham. Arnold had by now started his inspired Centre 42, and it was natural that he should visit us in Birmingham. I was beside myself with excitement. At last, I was to meet my hero. But the (now long-deceased) director of the Centre, a buffoon who would have denied both his undoubted conservatism and his antisemitism, suddenly and perversely banned me from coming anywhere near the meeting with Arnold, on pain of the sack.

It wasn't until the early 90s that I got to know Arnold. This began at a dramatists' seminar organised by David Edgar at Birmingham University, and soon developed into a relationship by correspondence. From time to time, he would exhort me to go and stay with him at his home in Hay-on-Wye – the National Portrait Gallery picture of him at his desk was taken there. 'I'll make you chopped liver, and we can go on long walks and chew the fat', he once wrote. To my regret, things somehow always got in the way, and I never took up his invitation.

When we won the Palme d'Or at Cannes for *Secrets And Lies*, his heartfelt letter of congratulation lamented wistfully and rather movingly that writing and directing movies is what he had always dreamed of doing, and that although he was delighted for me, he was also a little jealous. I think he adopted a kind of paternal attitude to me in a way, which was always charming, never patronising.

In fact, my long association with the London Film School – as student, tutor and chairman – owes something to Arnold: the first I ever knew of it was from the Penguin edition of his plays, which reported that he had attended the place. And it was only when he died that I learned that it was one of his tutors, Lindsay Anderson, who first brought his writing to the attention of the Royal Court Theatre, and that Arnold's son Lindsay is named after the director.

We saw each other in London occasionally, and after he moved to Hove with Dusty, we carried on our intermittent correspondence until he became too ill. He was constructively critical of my 'Jewish' play, *Two Thousand Years*, at the National Theatre, and when the same theatre announced my next play there, *Grief*, he complained, somewhat petulantly, that I was obviously unaware that he had written a one-woman opera with the same title, which had been performed once in Japan. Then we disagreed over my support for the ban on Israeli theatre company Habima's visit to London.

But the overriding thing about Arnold was that one could never be angry or irritated with him. Because whatever the issue was, you always knew that for him, it came from the heart; he was always motivated by that same honest, pure passion we'd all been so inspired by back in the late 1950s.

Arnold Wesker was a great writer and a lovely guy. It was a privilege to know him, but I wish I'd known him better.

'EMOTIONAL ARCHAEOLOGY': SECOND GENERATION JEWISH ARTISTS IN THE UK

MONICA BOHM-DUCHEN

The generation which experienced the profound upheavals and traumas of the rise of fascism, the Second World War and the Holocaust at first hand is on the cusp of disappearing. It is not surprising, then, that the compulsion felt by so many of their offspring to ensure that those experiences are not forgotten has become ever more urgent. As artist Ardyn Halter has written so eloquently:

> The lives of the murdered cry out against the convenience of oblivion … This is a baton, the survivor says to his children. And in tacit agreement that such a baton can indeed be handed on, they come to be called the Second Generation. This becomes their burden, whether willingly borne or thrust upon them, but intolerable. Necessary, but impossible.

The need to acknowledge and explore the distinctive position of those whom Helen Epstein dubbed the 'Children of the Holocaust' when setting out to find 'a group of people who, like me, were possessed by a history they had never lived' dates back to the mid-1970s. A more detailed academic scrutiny of the phenomenon now most commonly known as the 'Second Generation' (but also the 'hinge generation' and the 'generation after') and the concomitant concept of 'postmemory' (as well as the related concepts of 'vicarious memory', 'mémoire trouée', 'rememory' and 'prosthetic memory') gathered momentum in the 1990s and has shown little sign of abating.[6] Many of the examples highlighted in this essay suggest that the output of the past two decades has taken a bolder, more confident tone – often confronting family trauma in less circumspect ways than before.

Indeed, although it is too early to make any judgements on the matter, there is growing evidence that some artist members of the 'Third Generation' are also rising to the challenge of engaging creatively with difficult family pasts. And while only a few Third Generation artists are referenced in this essay, their work reveals a great deal of thematic continuity with their Second Generation predecessors.

Marianne Hirsch, who first coined the hugely influential (and now perhaps over-used) term 'postmemory' in an article on Art Spiegelman's graphic novel *Maus* in the early 1990s, has been exploring the concept ever since, and in 2012 defined it as follows:

> In my reading, postmemory is distinguished from memory by generational distance and from history by deep personal connection. Postmemory is a powerful and very particular form of memory precisely because its connection to its object or source is mediated not through recollection but through an imaginative investment and creation.

In a similar vein, Henri Raczymow, in *Contes d'exil et d'oubli* (*Tales of Exile and Forgetting*) has written of his concept of 'mémoire trouée' (memory with holes), first used in 1986, as follows: 'I try to restore a non-memory, which by definition cannot be filled in or recovered. … The world that was destroyed was not mine. I never knew it. But I am, so many of us are, the orphans of that world.' And Ardyn Halter puts it even more concisely when he writes of 'the cuckoo of another's memory within your nest'.

★★★

The creative responses of visual artists to their families' complicated and traumatic histories, however, have been distinctly neglected – and when they have been examined in any detail, by American-Jewish academics such as Hirsch, Dora Apel and Stephen C. Feinstein, the focus has tended to be on artists work-

---

6   1995 was the fiftieth anniversary of the end of the Second World War and acted as both a symbolic and psychological watershed.

ing in the USA. In Israel, where the topic of the Holocaust, in art and society alike, remained almost a taboo for many decades, scholarly attention has only relatively recently begun to focus on those visual artists who have grappled with its legacy. Nevertheless, claims such as this one by Batya Brutin corroborate what the American writers have also discovered: 'Many details from their parents' past are like a mystery that they must unravel. Since they cannot explore the subject directly with their parents, they do so through their imagination and their art.' And in Germany, as testified by publications such as *Bilder zum Judenmord* (2014), translated into English as *Judenmord: Art and the Holocaust in Post-war Germany*, attention has recently shifted from the art produced by the victims and their descendants to the art produced by the descendants of the perpetrators, sometimes known as *die Nachgeborenen* (those born after), a phrase disquietingly similar to the 'generation after'.

In other words, the work of Second Generation Jewish artists working in the UK – most of them, for historical reasons, the children of refugees from Nazism rather than Holocaust survivors – remains relatively uncharted territory. While I myself baulk at the application without distinction of the term 'survivor' to both these First Generation groups, there is no doubt that the Holocaust lies at the dark heart of the artworks produced by the descendants of both groups. And few, if any of them, would disagree with New York-based artist Ruth Liberman's assertion that:

In some way or other, the Holocaust has probably informed and inflected much of what I do. Yet even though I have worked with sources from the Holocaust I would not say that any of my work is *about* the Holocaust – none of the pieces make that claim. Many of my art projects are the fallout of having always known about the Holocaust, second-hand.

They would also undoubtedly concur with French-born, half-Jewish artist Christian Boltanski's statement that 'My work is not about, it is after.'

This oblique approach to the subject of the Holocaust has, perhaps, freed up artists enabling them to explore the subject from the perspective of both intimacy and distance, and allowing them to probe and reveal their material in often startling ways. Sometimes the artists utilise a variety of mediums, including film, photograms, site-specific activity and even tattoos to create work that is often bold and powerful and sometimes shocking and disturbing. Removed by time from the experiences their parents or grandparents have gone through, they are able to address – with a jolt or shudder – areas that might have been previously taboo.

***

While the responsibilities and creative challenges of making art in the shadow of the Holocaust are shared by at least two other notable artists currently working in this country – Venezuela-born Glenn Sujo and London-born David Breuer-Weil – their relationship with the topic is less directly autobiographical than that of the UK-based artists I am focusing on here. In Sujo's case, he bravely takes on the impossible task of depicting naked bodies in extremis; while Breuer-Weil's consciousness of being the son of a refugee from Nazism imbues everything he produces, but in a non-specific, iconographically complex and essentially allegorical fashion. For these reasons, while I greatly admire the works of both these artists, I have decided not to examine their work in any detail.

In this text, I will focus on artists whose work derives from a direct and very personal engagement with their own family histories, beginning with those who have chosen to use the traditional medium of painting as a means of expression and moving on to those who have embraced the more contemporary media of installation, montage and performance art, and ending with a brief discussion of those who have initiated more communal projects, involving those from similar backgrounds. Although made use of in a wide variety of ways, photographs – and precious pre-war family photographs above all – remain a pivotal reference point throughout, for reasons I will explore later. Also running as leitmotifs throughout the text are the following: the significance of gender, since it can hardly be accidental that all but one of the artists under discussion are female; and the painful power of silence, with the death of a close relative often leading to unexpected discoveries and a compulsion to find out more.

***

Let me start, then, with artists whose creative energies were most explicitly focused on Second Generation issues in the 1980s and 1990s. One of the first of these was the above-quoted Ardyn Halter, who works in Israel and the UK and whose Holocaust survivor father, Roman Halter (1927–2012), was also an artist. In the early 1980s, Ardyn created a moving series of eleven oil paintings (later turned into prints) under the collective title *The Family I Never Knew*, based on six small inter-war photographs, the only images that survived of his Polish-Jewish family. By his own admission, however, he found the photos 'frustratingly flat'. 'They [his relatives] live in the same way as still life. I could come no closer to them than to those photographs.' Halter first transposed the painfully uncommunicative images into paint in an emotionally impassive style and then (in some cases) surrounded and/or overlaid them with antisemitic slogans and euphemistic terminology such as 'fremd', 'lebensraum', 'umsiedlung', formed of the aggressive gothic script so popular during the Third Reich. Softer Hebrew lettering was used to give the names of family members and their dates of death. The final artworks vividly convey a craving for an intimacy forever thwarted by the Nazis' genocidal policies. As the artist puts it:

> In several of the paintings from the series *The Family I Never Knew* I employed lettering, slogans that are suspended, like a veil, between me/the viewer and the subject. These formal devices indicate distance, an abyss I cannot cross, do not wish to cross, the limits to my experience, the distinction between knowledge and inherited knowledge.

In Halter's later work in painting and stained glass (when he sometimes collaborated with his father), the references and imagery, often drawn from biblical sources, are less obviously personal and generally more optimistic – even when in the early 2000s, he was commissioned to produce two windows for the new National Genocide Memorial Centre in Kigali (entitled *Descent to Genocide* and *The Way Forward*). Significantly though, Ardyn has only recently felt able to articulate in words the profound ambivalence he still feels about his position as Roman's son, in the form of an eloquent and achingly frank soon-to-be-published manuscript entitled *The Fire and the Bonfire*, which he started writing in 2004 but revised considerably after his father's death.

Another artist whose earlier output is more obviously relevant to this essay than the work she has produced since then is London-based painter Julie Held. Both her parents came to England as refugees before the war, but as was so often the case, spoke little about their earlier lives and the families left behind who perished. Unspoken but inherited grief was hugely compounded for Held by the protracted ill health and early death of her mother (a talented sculptor) in 1966 when the artist was only 18 years old. In the early 1990s, she embarked on a series of richly coloured, unashamedly expressionistic compositions, such as *Commemoration* (c. 1993), *The Dinner Party* (1996) and *The Supper* (1996) featuring communal dining tables profoundly haunted by absence even when peopled, since while some of the figures depicted are family members recalled from childhood, others are members of the family in Europe she never knew.

In the early 2000s the references to Held's family history became more oblique, in the form of enticing yet also unsettling images of shops, and shoe shops in particular, often with the artist herself looking in from outside. There are multiple references here: to the artist's longstanding awareness of a tension between inside and outside in her own life; to the fact that one of her grandfathers owned a department store in Germany; and to her mother's love of shoes as well as their symbolic resonance as a means of stepping into different roles.

Moreover, for many years around the time of her mother's birthday, Held produced what she terms a 'posthumous portrait', evoking in paint an imaginary process of ageing, which must have helped keep the memory of her mother alive but at the same time acts as a painful reminder of absence and loss. She also produced several intensely moving imaginary double portraits of her parents together. Towards the end of her father's life, she began to depict him too, in dignified, tender but unflinching images of old age and gradual physical diminishment.

Susie Mendelsson, now primarily a sculptor but who (like Held) for many years worked in a painterly, expressionist mode more closely allied to a Germanic tradition than a British one, has also used the motif of the dining table as an eloquent metaphor for familial absences. In her case, this formed part of a more diverse body of work, most of them following the death in 2000 of her father Wolfgang (Walter), who arrived in England from Germany at the age of 8 in 1939 on a Kindertransport. In the artist's own words:

> My father was an Anglophile who loved churches, particularly medieval ones. … He also had a fascination with death and loved to visit graveyards … He was a quiet man, and during his life he was a source of mystery. His death allowed me to explore the complexities of his personality … I can now let the memories of my father rest in peace … The paintings are enigmatic and atmospheric, showing an individual man amongst crowds of people. Full of humanity, the paintings draw on medieval and church imagery, as well as war.

As well as a series of large paintings collectively titled *In Honour of my Father*, which focus primarily on his preoccupation with Christian art and architecture, between 1999 and 2003, Mendelsson produced other works on related themes, notably *Home Life*, in which 'the head of the family sits in his familiar armchair, disconnected from home life'; *Daddy's Busy, I Can't See You* ('my father had a small office in our house filled with books … increasingly the books and papers seemed to be gobbling him up. He was slowly disappearing and there was no room for me') and *Destination Unknown* ('I often try to imagine what it felt like to be on a worn-out train, perhaps a cattle truck, being carted off to an unknown destination').

In the paintings produced in the 1990s by Marlene Rolfe, many of them apparently naturalistic portraits but with strongly symbolic elements, she conveys the uneasiness of her position as both daughter and mother – most memorably expressed in *Family* (1990). This uneasiness was inextricably bound up with her awareness of her mother's and her aunt's past, which is dealt with more explicitly in other paintings such as *Wandervögel* (1993). Her mother, Ilse, born into an assimilated Berlin Jewish family, had been active in the German Communist Party and spent three years as a political prisoner in concentration camps before her release in 1938, when she emigrated to England and later married a 'terribly English' non-Jew. Her mother's twin sister, Else, a Social Democrat, was also imprisoned and released, escaping to Norway and then New York. Initially, Rolfe knew virtually nothing of her mother's history but with the 'old age, frailty and death of [her] mother and aunt,' she felt an increasingly urgent need 'to recreate the lost worlds of their past and of [her] own childhood'.

★★★

Other artists started grappling with the legacy of their parents' histories in the 1990s and continue to do so. One example is Brighton-based Barbara Loftus, who was born in 1946 to Hildegard, a German-Jewish refugee mother and a lapsed Irish Catholic, communist and anti-Zionist father – who seems to have been unwilling or unable to engage with his wife's traumas. Hildegard had come to England in 1939 as a refugee from Nazi Germany and had tried to obtain visas for her family to escape. However, she was too late; the war started and her family, trapped in Germany, were eventually transported to Auschwitz, where they perished. She was the family's sole survivor. Barbara only became fully aware of her mother's experiences in the mid-1990s when Hildegard was already 85 years old. 'We were at home together,' the artist has related, 'just the two of us. She was looking at the china cabinet next to us and then she started to talk about the day the SA came to confiscate the porcelain, and I was so shocked I just felt a responsibility to do something.'

This revelation marked the start of an ongoing compulsion to engage as an artist with her mother's story, beginning by recording the latter's reminiscences, not long before her health declined and made it impossible to do so. The first body of work Loftus produced was *A Confiscation of Porcelain*, which was completed in 1996 but revisited and reworked in ever more pared-down ways in 2010–11. The work is a series of meticulously crafted, apparently realist, psychologically taut paintings recreating that pivotal moment in November 1938 when Hildegard was 9 years old and the seemingly safe, emphatically 'feminine', bourgeois domesticity of her home was so rudely ruptured. The paintings were preceded by exquisite preparatory drawings and extensive historical research, and followed by an artist's book and a short film – a pattern that would establish itself in the related projects that followed, but with the filmic element gaining in importance.

Her *German Landscape with Wandervogel* series (begun in 2000), painted in a deliberately dry realist style reminiscent of nineteenth-century Nordic renderings of forested terrain, references a romantic 'back to nature' youth movement popular in interwar Germany to which her mother had enthusiastically belonged. That aspects of the Wandervögel movement were appropriated all too easily by the Nazis and absorbed into their toxic ideology, is the unspoken subtext of this intentionally disquieting project. This was followed by another narrative cycle, entitled *Sigismund's Watch: A Tiny Catastrophe* (completed in 2007). This focuses on a relatively minor but symbolically loaded domestic incident during Hildegard's childhood when, unbeknown to her parents, she witnessed her mother smashing her father's fob watch during a violent argument fuelled by the economic hardships they, like many other families, were suffering during the Weimar period.

More recently, although Loftus continues to work as a painter, she has increasingly turned her attention to the medium of film, producing *Lieder ohne Worte* (*Songs without Words*, 2013) and *Across the Land and the Water: the Two Journeys of the Family Basch* (2018), a poetic amalgam of voiceover, original artworks, family photographs and archival film footage. As the artist explains, the two journeys in question are 'Hildegard's – west to the safety of England – and the ultimate journey east, of the family she left behind in Berlin'.

Another film project, *Prussian Blue*, is currently in the pipeline, described by Loftus as a 'lyrical speculation on time, power and the visualisation of memory', 'a work of creative and psychological restitution'. She is also working on a new publication entitled *Before they Perished: Visualisations of Respectability*, 'which develops further the story of my post-memory experience of my mother Hildegard's life between 1920 and 1942'. Tellingly, it will contain an essay by Lutz Winckler in which he proposes that her 'perspective is that of a "displaced" person, belonging neither fully in England nor in Germany, whose "home" is the in-between space of the studio, where an identity can be given form'.

★★★

Other UK artists have similarly used the form of short 'essay films' to express the elusiveness and ultimate unknowability of their parents' experiences. Recent examples include Caroline Pick's *Home Movie* (2013); Anthea Kennedy's and Ian Wiblin's *The View from our House* (2013) and *Four Parts of a Folding Screen* (2018); Marina Willer's *Red Trees* (2017); and Sarah Dobai's *The Donkey Field* (still in progress as I write). Increasingly used in film criticism to describe 'a self-reflective and self-referential documentary cinema that blurs the lines between fiction and nonfiction', the term 'essay film' was coined by Hans Richter, in 1940, as a mode that 'allows the filmmaker to transgress the rules and parameters of the traditional documentary practice, granting the imagination with all its artistic potentiality free reign [sic]' – a definition that certainly holds true for all the films cited above.

★★★

In stark contrast to the emphatically figurative, carefully researched and considered approach of Loftus, Ruth Rix, born in England in 1942 to German-born artist Helga Michie (1921–2018), employs an open-ended, quasi-abstract but suggestive repertoire of forms which allow for multiple interpretations. The titles (such as *Secret Ground* and *House*) of her raw, gestural, unequivocally tactile canvases are allusive and enigmatic too. But when Rix talks of her profound need to bridge the gaps between the present and 'a past that suddenly stopped', the relevance of her position as a child of war and dislocation lends her work an extra layer of significance and poignancy. Recurrent motifs such as a solitary black dog, the outline of a rudimentary building, an exterior staircase with an iron railing, come to speak eloquently of unsettledness and wandering – as Rix herself has put it bluntly, 'a lot of transience'.

Rix's daughter Rebecca Swift is also an artist – a member of the so-called 'Third Generation' – who chooses to engage with her family history in a very different way. Mention should be made of an installation entitled *Staircase* (2000), in which all three generations were involved. This installation and associated performance drew not only on the family's pre-war history in Vienna, the impact of the Second World War and the Holocaust, but also on Ruth's relationship to that history, with Rebecca acting as the creator and facilitator of the overall concept.

Yorkshire-based artist Judith Tucker is the daughter of Berlin-born writer Eva Tucker (1929-2015), author of two memoirs, *Berlin Mosaic* (2005) and *Becoming English* (2009). Abstracted and implicitly symbolic landscape forms have long been the primary focus of Tucker's art. Coastlines, in particular, fascinate her, as the emblem of possibilities of 'passage and displacement, of arrivals and departures and not of permanent dwelling'. In the early 2000s she came to realise their deeper significance for her and, intent on investigating the hitherto-neglected relationship between landscape painting and Second Generation memory, embarked on a number of projects exploring the creative and intellectual potential of what she has termed 'postmemorial landscape'.

Inspired by photographs in her grandmother's album of her mother and grand-parents on the beach at Ahlbeck on the north coast of Germany in the early 1930s, Tucker made a trip there in 2003. Once a popular resort, Ahlbeck was now 'an evocative mixture of decay and lavish restoration set against the vast flatness of the Baltic'. Her imagination was caught by the *Strandkörbe* still characteristic of the region – a hooded beach lounger that is somewhere between a beach hut and a deckchair – which provided her with a potent symbol for human absence and the passage of time. In her own words, they 'offer the possibility of shelter' but standing empty, 'have a melancholy timbre'. First exhibited in 2004, the series of relatively naturalistic drawings and more abstracted paintings that resulted were tersely and tellingly entitled *Resort*.

Another body of work exploring the significance of liminal spaces directly connected to Tucker's family history followed soon after. *Tense* (2008) was also prompted by a series of pre-war photographs from her grandmother's album. This time the setting was a forest resort, Friedrichroda in Thüringia. The photographs she found most intriguing were those of a swimming pool, which evoked not only the fact that her grandmother had trained to be a gymnast but also the Nazis' toxic obsession with the healthy body. 'Thus my images of the pool, these images of spaces of pleasure and leisure, are contaminated by association.'

A third series of images followed, called *Spectres on the Beach*, focusing on the Danish island of Bornholm, popular with German tourists in the interwar years, and once again inspired by 'some yellowing photographs' in her grandmother's album. 'People often smile in holiday photos, perhaps sending good memories into the unknown future; this becomes all the more poignant when we know with hindsight what that future was. I speculate with dark thoughts: perhaps they chose a Danish resort because of rising antisemitism in Germany.' On a visit to the island in 2010 she was struck by the physical legacy of its wartime occupation, first by the Germans then by the Russians. She notes some 'lumps of concrete barely indistinguishable from the rocks', that are the remains of a U-boat station: 'In the dunes … are larger more complete concrete structures, one is a rocket launcher.' The proximity of these sinister remnants to sites of leisure understandably fired her imagination.

Although Tucker is distinctly more au fait and directly engaged with theoretical issues than most of the other artists under discussion here, any potential dryness of approach is more than offset by her technical skill and inventiveness, and the tactile, almost sensual properties of much of her work. As I wrote some years ago, ideas 'are so completely embodied in the physicality of the painted surface, that medium and message become inseparable'. Tucker has observed that there is a conceptual aspect to this too: 'The surfaces operate both as enticement and sometimes as a screen preventing one from seeing.'

★★★

Between 1999 and 2013, London-based Sara Davidmann focused mainly on photographing and carrying out oral history recordings in collaboration with people from transgender and queer communities in the UK. Since 2011, however, she has increasingly focused on her own family and family history. *My Mother's Notebooks* (2011) comprises a series of close-up photographs taken of time-worn pages from the eponymous notebooks, discovered only when her mother had to move into a nursing home.

In Davidmann's own words:

[nothing] prepared me for the vast quantity of handwritten personal notebooks and diaries stored in cardboard boxes, and bound notes and envelopes piled in the garage and secreted in cupboards in every room of the house ... In sorting through my mother's paperwork, I began to photograph her notebooks in the rooms in which I found them. The photographs in this series tell the story of my parent's marriage and my mother's attempts to come to terms with repercussions from my father's childhood... [of] how she came to understand that my father's experiences in Nazi Berlin led to his mental health deteriorating, and how she struggled to keep the family together.

Davidmann is currently working on a new project based on her German-Jewish family history, to be exhibited under the title *My Name is Sara*, and even more directly predicated on her father's inability to deal with a traumatic past:

My father, Manfred, and his sister Susi survived the Holocaust by escaping from Berlin on the Kindertransport, arriving in the UK in 1939 at the respective ages of 14 and 17 ...These experiences formed a space in his life that was too painful to revisit and I grew up knowing very little about the Jewish side of my family history.

Three years ago, however, she discovered an album of photographs and handwritten notes in German. With the help of the Wiener Library and the Arolsen Archives, the artist embarked on a 'search for traces of their lives', which revealed the terrible truth that 'family members were deported to, and murdered, in concentration camps at Auschwitz and Theresienstadt. Others survived by escaping to Shanghai, France and Israel, and by living hidden in Berlin with false documents.'

At the same time as conducting this research, Davidmann embarked on a series of photographic works which make conceptually complex but poignant – and sometimes shocking – reference to her father's experiences. One of these is *Wearing my father's clothing*, which reproduces a photograph, taken in 1957, depicting the artist as a child wearing her father's striped pyjamas: 'In the context of this project the pyjamas look like a concentration camp uniform. ... In one sense I have spent my life wearing my father's clothing.'

My Name is Sara consists of six hand-printed photograms on resin-coated paper, which incorporate a plait of the artist's hair, cut off when she was 5 years old and kept as a memento by her mother. As Davidmann explains:

> With photograms, light is shone on, or through, an object placed on photographic paper in a dark room. The object's resistance to the light is what essentially makes the photograph. When the photogram is printed, the area of resistance – the area where the object was – retains the white of the paper while the areas touched by light become black.
>
> The first photogram was made with the plait inside the envelope. Gradually I unravelled the plait, which had been tightly curled, held in the same position, for many years. In an early version of this artwork I included a high contrast black and white image of my great grandmother Dorothea's transportation papers to Theresienstadt. On this document the name 'Sara' had been written ... and then crossed out by hand. I assume this must have been done when the papers were discovered by someone who objected to the addition of a name forced on the women by the Nazis. The scoring through of the name is poignant. There had been so many crossings out – so many erasures.

The final images – ghostly, disembodied, floating luminously in a sea of black – are subtle, allusive and suggestive. They are all the more resonant for not being literal or explicit in their multiple references to the tragic associations both of the subject of hair in a Holocaust context and of the name Sara.

Three other works in this series incorporate less orthodox materials and techniques. *Mischling* ('half-breed' or 'mixed race', the term used by the Nazis to categorise people who had one or two Jewish grandparents) consists of luridly coloured photographs taken under a microscope of blood from members of Davidmann's family. The photographs are exhibited in the form of twelve lightboxes to enhance their luminosity. The other two works take their cue from the photo album mentioned earlier and use an experimental process known as a chemigram. *Looking for Leo* derives from a photograph of the artist's great-uncles, Leo and Arthur, taken at the German seaside in 1924, both of whom 'disappeared in the Holocaust' and *Kinderfest* is based on a photograph of a children's party taken in 1923 – the poignancy of this goes almost without saying.

After making a digital negative from the original photograph, the artist used chemicals as well as her own blood to intervene in the process of developing both images, thus:

> Creating a direct connection between the artist, the past as it is perceived through the photograph, and the continuation of the family bloodline. Layers of darkroom chemicals and blood, photographic bleach, and drawing and scratching on the surface were used to simultaneously erase and reveal the original images. Bleach disrupted and transformed the photographs in unpredictable and uncontrollable ways.

The resulting images are both startling and unsettling.

Lily Markiewicz, born in post-war Germany to two Holocaust survivors, but based in the UK since the early 1980s, has evolved an understated, oblique but powerful symbolic vocabulary with which to explore the complex nature of post-Holocaust female identity. Since the 1990s she has concentrated mainly on large-scale photo-based installations, which often include elements of video and sound. Although a secular Jew with a sophisticated grasp of feminist, psychoanalytical and linguistic theory, much of her work – for example, *Silence Woke Me Up Today* (1989) and the pointedly-titled installation *I Don't Celebrate Christmas* (1990) – contains allusions to traditional Jewish practices.

In the installation *Places to Remember*, produced in the early 1990s and based on her slightly earlier artist's book *The Price of Words/Places to Remember 1–26*, fragmented black and white images of sand flowing through hands and into a bowl are accompanied by a cyclical, ambient sound recording of the artist's own voice, in which she alludes in poetic ways to issues of dislocation and alienation. By the unexpected and abrupt inclusion of the word 'Jew', however, she anchors the cryptic generalisations in a highly specific context – that of a member of the Second Generation attempting to come to terms with the legacy of the Holocaust.

In Markiewicz's own words:

> My work is about dis/placement, especially in relation to culture, language and territory … my images are of the most basic familiars (sand, water, naked bodies), located in local familiars (parks, pools, homes) … What I present may potentially be recognised, yet it is also quite foreign; something one may be drawn to yet is also frightened of. As much as I create spaces the viewer can enter into, I also deny access to the very space that is created – thus inviting

hesitation, doubt and ambivalence, but also considerations about dwelling in general, and belonging in particular.

She continues: 'The most appropriate metaphors to describe my working process come from the fields of archaeology, anthropology and psychoanalysis.'

Tellingly, the website of photographer and anthropologist Julia Winckler is prefaced by a quotation from Nigerian-born writer Ben Okri's *Birds of Heaven*: 'The artist [as] a conduit through which lost things are recovered.' Winckler knew virtually nothing of the Jewish side of her family history until 1998 when she moved into her great-aunt's house. In the attic she discovered an old leather suitcase belonging to her great-aunt's Jewish husband Hugo Hecker, which had accompanied him on his journey to England in 1939; she also found two small photographs of Hugo's family, the only other trace of a past of which he never spoke. Julia's determination to 'break through this silence' gave rise to *Traces* (1998–2002) a series of forty photographic images in three parts.

The first part, 'Witnessing', draws primarily on those two surviving photographs; the second, 'Searching', comprises evocative photographs Winckler took on a journey to Poland in 2001 when she visited the Hecker family's hometown as well as sites of (tragic) Jewish significance in and near Krakow. The third part, 'Preserving', as the name suggests, is about 'holding onto objects and documents for their potential to provide testimony'. The still photographs were followed in 2002 by a film of the same name made in collaboration with Nerea Martinez de Lecca.

Shortly after this, Winckler embarked on a tripartite project, entitled *Two Sisters*, which confronted the challenges of coming from a largely non-Jewish German family background by investigating the dramatically different life stories of her grandmother Viktoria Otto and her great-aunt Martha Hecker. Between 1943 and 1944 Viktoria worked as a secretary for the German central railway authority in Berlin, later claiming to be haunted by images of Jews being deported to the East. Martha came to the UK as a domestic servant and was interned as an 'enemy alien' first in Holloway Prison and then on the Isle of Man, where she met her future husband. On her release she joined the ATS as a lorry driver. Winckler's work is driven by her 'desire to grasp memories and at the same time reflect on the inaccuracy of memory'.

In more recent years, like quite a few of the artists featured in this essay, Winckler has turned her attention away from her immediate family to focus on projects dealing with other kinds of experiences and memories. Nevertheless, nearly all her work of the past twenty years has been underpinned by an urge to investigate 'archival traces within the context of collective memory and migration narratives', to probe 'how neglected archival sources can reveal forgotten histories of great significance to our understanding of the present'.

***

As the daughter of two Holocaust survivors, Somerset-based Lorna Brunstein's connection to a deeply traumatic past is intimate and inescapable. For over twenty years, Brunstein has been making work born of her experience of being the child of survivors. As she has written:

> As a Second Generation Holocaust Survivor I am trying to make sense of my family's past, exploring issues of identity, memory, loss, and displacement. I am interested in family histories, memorials, testimonies and the silences we all carry and have been shaped by. The notion of inherited trauma is at the core of my work. My practice has a forensic dimension, an emotional archaeology in which traces, fragments and memories are the starting point ... My work intends to give the viewer a transformative and immersive experience and aims to create a tension and energy within a contemplative space.

After Auschwitz, a haunting mixed media installation of 2019, grew out of two visits to Auschwitz, which her mother Esther survived but her grandmother Sara did not. The trips, which took place in 2017 and 2018, were organised by the Unite Against Fascism (UAF) campaign group as part of their annual educational programme:

> In the year of my mother's death, I made a return trip to Auschwitz with my youngest daughter Alicia. We stood at that same selection point, as mother and daughter, remembering where in August 1944, both mother and daughter had also stood. It was a profound moment to be in that very bleak place, surrounded by ghosts, a place of unspeakable horror and yet it was also strangely uplifting – an affirmation of life. To go back as survivors, to carry the legacy, to remember, and to stand proud.

A key component of the installation, made in collaboration with her partner Richard White and with Alicia was soil gathered as a symbolically loaded act from the soles of shoes worn by members of the UAF group during those visits. Photographs of those same soles also featured in the installation, while dim lighting and a low altar-like table further contributed to the creation of a quasi-religious, ritualised environment.

Together, Lorna and Richard have also been active devising and leading what they term participatory 'performative walks'. The first of these was *Forced Walks: Honouring Esther*, which (uncomfortably and perhaps problematically) retraced her mother's journey from a German slave labour camp to Bergen-Belsen by transposing the route onto the English countryside. The second, *Sara's Last Steps*, will trace the final steps of a Jewish mother (the artist's grandmother) forcibly parted from her children at the Auschwitz selection point, transposed to the Lake District. The walk traverses the site of Calgarth housing estate near Windermere, which in 1945 was partly requisitioned for a group of child Holocaust survivors, known variously as 'The Boys' (of whom Lorna's Uncle Perec was one) and 'the Windermere Children'. Planned to mark the 75th anniversary of the arrival of those children but postponed due to Covid-19, *Sara's Last Steps* forms part of a cycle of work entitled 'Sanctuary' and 'Exile', commissioned by the Lake District Holocaust Project and intended to culminate in an installation in Windermere.

The temptations and pitfalls of over-identification are demonstrated even more forcibly in the work of Yishay Garbasz. Born in Israel in 1970, she lived and studied for a while in the UK and is now based in Berlin. Garbasz only discovered, at the age of 18, that her mother had been born in Germany when she had to provide details of her family background for an application form for the Israeli army: 'Yet even then, we did not break our habit of silence about the Holocaust.'

In my Mother's Footsteps (2003–9) comprises a series of photographs, later published in book form, which charts the journeys Garbasz took in 2000, over the space of a year, to trace her mother's journeys: from her birthplace in Berlin to her escape to Holland, deportation aged 14 to Westerbork, then Theresienstadt, Auschwitz, Christianstadt, the death march and finally Bergen-Belsen, where she and her two sisters were liberated. The accompanying texts were taken from an account written by her mother in the mid-1990s at the urging of the artist's father on his deathbed. As Garbasz put it:

> I needed to see firsthand what remained of my mother's memories. My mother left parts of her soul in those places, and I intended to go back to collect them. I could only do this through intimate familiarity with the locations. And as I trained in photography, the camera was going to be a tool to help me see.

The decision to use an old-fashioned, large-format camera, moreover, forced her to spend a substantial amount of time at each location, planning the image in advance.

In *The Numbers Project* (2011), Garbasz goes much further. Branding her mother's Auschwitz number on her left arm, true to size and in exactly the same place, she photographed it in a variety of different social contexts as the skin began to heal and also produced a video of the branding process itself. Significantly, her mother had had the tattoo removed while living in England, as 'she could not stand to answer the questions people kept asking her about her number. When my mother died, the number that she could not bear to see and have, I would see and have. I did not want to forget it or allow it to disappear from social consciousness.' Garbasz, who is transgender, has also explored issues of identity relating to her sexual reassignment surgery by documenting her body in the process of transformation, observing that 'for people who also are trans, it is our basic humanity that is challenged'.

While no British-born member of the Second Generation has to my knowledge gone to such extreme lengths to identify with a parent, mention should be made of the Russian-born grandchild of survivors, US-based artist Marina Vainshtein, who in the 1990s took it upon herself to have her entire body tattooed with elaborate imagery pertaining to the Holocaust. And in Israel, where it is still relatively unusual for a visual artist to confront the Holocaust-mediated mother-daughter relationship head-on, Rachel Nemesh is conspicuous for her recent large-scale portrayals of her (often naked) self and her elderly survivor mother intimately and suffocatingly bound together.

★★★

Based in the north of England, Jenny Kagan had a thirty-year-long career as a lighting designer for the theatre behind her when she changed course and, after studying architecture and drawing, decided to work as an independent artist. Her parents Joseph and Margaret Kagan met in the Kaunas Ghetto when her mother was just 17, and miraculously managed to survive the war, hiding for nine months in a wooden box with the help of a local man called Vytautas. In the artist's own words, 'I grew up with bedtime stories about their time in hiding in what they referred to as "the box". I consider myself lucky that they spoke often and openly about their experiences; many survivors did not.'

Kagan's creative response to her parents' experiences took the form of an ambitious and unashamedly theatrical, interactive installation called *Out of Darkness* (2016), shown in the atmospheric, subterranean Viaduct Theatre in Halifax. By her own admission, she is 'primarily interested in curating the moment of encounter. In surprising, delighting and inviting her audience to engage in new ways.' Visitors were invited to make their way through a darkened space to discover, among other things, a maze of barbed wire, seemingly solid windows which revealed images when illuminated, and suitcases that contained yet more elements of her parents' story. The installation, which also incorporated music and other sound effects, culminated in a poetic starscape.

While the primary inspiration for *Out of Darkness* was clearly the remarkable story of her parents' wartime experiences, Kagan is intent on pointing out that 'this is a show about memory and experience rather than about hard historical fact'. On one level this is an intensely romantic story, related with a humour and warmth that counteracts the brutal realities of life under Nazi occupation.

Jenny Stolzenberg (1947–2016) was the daughter of a Viennese-Jewish father who survived both Dachau and Buchenwald before managing to get to England. Like so many, he rarely spoke about his experiences. Only some years after his death in 1990 did Stolzenberg visit Auschwitz, where the piles of victims' belongings (shoes, spectacles and suitcases) made an indelible impact on her. She was also inspired by Primo Levi's description in *If This Is a Man* of the cruel ritual of 'the changing of the shoes', in which prisoners had just seconds to grab some footwear from a pile, resulting in them having to endure wearing ill-fitting, mismatched pairs which could nevertheless help prolong their lives.

Forgive and Do Not Forget (2002), titled in homage to her father's frequent exhortation, is Stolzenberg's best-known work. It is a powerful sculptural installation comprising a long procession of dozens of meticulously hand-crafted ceramic shoes – men's, women's and children's – many of them odd pairs. Modelled on the styles of the period, the shoes individualise the victims and allude only obliquely to the horror of genocide, resulting in a work of almost unbearably poignancy. While the work's primary reference is to the Nazi Holocaust, its resonances are far broader, as evidenced by the way it has been received in the diverse venues in which it has been exhibited.

For some years, printmaker Monica Petzal, born in London to German-Jewish refugee parents, conducted life story interviews for the British Library, focusing on eminent figures in the British art world, many of them émigrés. Increasingly, though, she has 'focused on my own family and their complicated and often untold stories, though I was too late to record them in person'. In 2013, a stint working in a print studio in Dresden (where her mother's family had lived before the war) resulted in a series of graphic works entitled *Indelible Marks: the Dresden Project*, and also led to her close involvement with the Dresden Trust, a charity that works towards reconciliation between Britain and Saxony (and Dresden and Coventry in particular).

Petzal started working on another ambitious print series in 2017, based on ideas that, she says, 'have been in gestation all my life'. Pointedly titled *Dissent and Displacement: A Modern Story*, the exhibition opened at Leicester

City Museum in February 2020 but was sadly curtailed by the Covid-19 pandemic. The series comprises six groups of large-scale, iconographically complex montage images which incorporate family photographs and archival material, painted elements and text to create lithographic prints which tell 'modern stories of opposition, persecution and persistence'. One such story is that of the Hess family, uprooted from Erfurt to Leicester, and whose magnificent private collection formed the basis of what is the finest ensemble of modern German art in this country.

Natasha Kerr originally worked as a commercial textile designer while beginning to experiment with using photographs to create fine art pieces. In 1994, her mother gave her a number of family photograph albums that had previously 'languished in plastic bags in an under stair cupboard' and which 'provided a visual thread that linked her to her unknown family history'. *At the End of the Day* of 2007 pays homage to her grandfather, a surgeon from Vienna who came to Britain in 1936. Interned as an 'enemy alien' during the Second World War, he was released to carry out essential medical work. The transfer print, incorporating silk screen, hand painting and hand-stitched linen, depicts him reclining on a blanket in a garden; Kerr's grandmother sits alongside, shielding her eyes from the sun, while an empty chair, a motif redolent of both displacement and absence, completes the picture. The pieces of stitched fabric radiate outwards from the image, suggestive (if only semi-consciously) of an optimistically non-specific, colourful flag form.

This very personal work prompted other families, as well as a variety of public and commercial bodies, to commission Kerr to incorporate their own stories within a similarly handcrafted mixed media artwork. Kerr's aim remains the distillation of the life story of one particular individual, evoking a bittersweet nostalgia for a past accessible now only by bringing together different fragments, even when the story in question is a relatively untroubled one. Although Kerr is officially Third Generation, certain leitmotifs remain constant – above all, the silences that prevail in families with a dark and troubled past, the discovery of a hitherto unknown family history through family photograph albums and the artist's attempt to make use of 'visual threads' to establish a personal if fragile link with that history.

Some artists have gone a step further and encouraged other people with similar backgrounds, not necessarily professional artists, to collaborate on communal projects. A notable example of this is the *Memory Quilt* project, initiated by artists Julia Burton and Rosalind Gelbart, Second Generation members of the '45 Aid Society, which raises funds to support survivors and children's charities and to promote Holocaust education.

The idea for the quilt originated as the group planned for the 70th anniversary of the liberation of the camps, which was to be marked in 2015. Inspired by Sheree Charalampous' dementia quilt and the NAMES Project AIDS Memorial Quilt, conceived in the USA in 1985, Burton and Gelbart came up with the idea of commemorating every one of the above-mentioned 'Windermere Boys' in the form of four large wall hangings.

Each survivor's family was asked to create a square image on a piece of white cotton fabric to represent the survivor and their story, incorporating significant objects or photographs relating to that individual. The quilts also include several maps of central Europe, with the names of the survivors symbolically inscribed onto their countries of origin. A large-format book, illustrating all the individual squares as well as the completed quilts and accompanied by explanatory texts, has also been produced.

More recently still, artist and educator Caroline Slifkin (not herself the child or grandchild of refugees or survivors but descended from a Jewish family that settled in the UK around the turn of the twentieth century) has initiated another communal project, entitled *Keepsakes of the Kindertransport/Holocaust*. Prompted in part by the Covid-19 lockdown and the way it has encouraged us to 'reflect, revisit and share stories and experiences with each other', she has invited members of the Second and Third Generations from around the world to create individual two-dimensional pieces, no bigger than A4 in size, that will be brought together in the form of a collaborative art book. Materials can include 'any drawing, painting, written words, quotes, mixed media, collage, and copies of photographs and documents'.

The urge to remember and reconstitute family histories by recourse to both visual and verbal sources clearly remains a compelling one. But as Ardyn Halter astutely observed: 'I am troubled by art or literature on the Shoah that is itself not troubled by its own endeavour'. An awareness of the impossibility of the task lies – or should lie – at the very heart of every attempt.

★★★

Notwithstanding the wide range of artistic styles and media employed by the artists under discussion, and the differing levels of explicitness in terms of their engagement with the field of memory studies, the preoccupations they share are remarkably consistent. And this is despite the fact that their birthdates range from the 1940s to the 1970s and that not all are fully Jewish. When Lorna Brunstein describes her work as embodying 'an emotional archaeology in which traces, fragments and memories are the starting point', she could well be speaking for all of them.

As we have seen, family photographs, nearly always few in number and which often only come to light after a relative's death, exercise a particular, almost talismanic fascination. Photographs, often taken in the present by the artists themselves, of locations associated with their parents' pre-war and wartime lives are another recurring preoccupation. Again and again, a recourse to photographs helps counter the overwhelming silences about a traumatic past so prevalent in the families of survivors and refugees. As Marianne Hirsch puts it so eloquently, 'Photographs in their enduring "umbilical" connection to life are precisely the medium connecting first- and second-generation remembrance, memory and postmemory. They are the leftovers, the fragmentary sources and building blocks, shot through with holes, of the work of postmemory.'

And then there is the issue of gender, since readers cannot fail to have noticed that virtually all the artists I have mentioned (with no prior intention on my part) are female. The reasons for this may well include the peculiar intimacy (not necessarily desired) of the mother and daughter dyad; the woman as bearer both of children and memory; the related fact that it is the matriarchal line which determines whether a child is Jewish, according to halachic (Jewish religious) law, and the perception of the domestic sphere as a poignant microcosm of the wider world. Once again, Hirsch provides food for thought:

> I certainly do not want to go so far as to argue that memory is neatly differentiated by gender, or by other categories of social difference. But I do see the preoccupation with memory, and especially the memory of those populations who have been left out of the archives of official histories, as rooted in movements for social change such as feminism ... Feminist approaches allow me to bring the entangled strands of disparate traumatic histories into more intimate contact.

I would go further and argue that it is not just feminism that can act as a spur, but the creative act itself, that 'imaginative investment' which enables artists not only to process their complex emotions in relation to their family pasts but through their artworks to communicate those emotions to others. 'Familial postmemory' thus morphs into what has been termed 'affiliative memory'. As Judith Tucker has put it, 'In a way, there is a paradox here for those of us who are second-generation artists: the overwhelming nature of the traumatic events can simultaneously overshadow and stimulate a search to articulate our own experience.' We might recall too Lily Markiewicz's claim that 'to make art is to "make home"', and the comment made about Barbara Loftus that for her '"home" is the in-between space of the studio, where an identity can be given form'.

Last but by no means least, it is striking how many of the artists have felt compelled to engage with different traumatic pasts (among them slavery and the Rwandan and Bosnian genocides) – intent on making others aware there should never be a hierarchy of suffering. Also noteworthy (as in the work of a much younger Third Generation artist, Gideon Summerfield) is the way so many of these artists view their engagement with their own family histories as a natural path towards empathy and solidarity with migrants, refugees and survivors of atrocities in the present.

APPENDIX 1: BIBLIOGRAPHY

Key texts

Apel, Dora, *Memory Effects: The Holocaust and the Art of Secondary Witnessing* (Rutgers University Press, 2002)

Bohm-Duchen, Monica, and Grodzinski, Vera (eds.), *Rubies and Rebels: Jewish Female Identity in Contemporary British Art* (Lund Humphries, 1996)

Brutin, Batya 'Artists: "Second Generation" in Israel', 2009 (available at https://jwa.org/encyclopedia/article/artists-second-generation-in-israel)

Epstein, Helen, *Children of the Holocaust: Conversations with Sons and Daughters of Survivors* (G.P. Putnam, 1979)

Feinstein, Stephen C. (ed.), *Witness And Legacy: Contemporary Art About the Holocaust* (Lerner Publishing Group, 1995)

Feinstein, Stephen C. (ed.), *Absence/Presence: Essays and Reflections on the Artistic Memory of the Holocaust – Religion, Theology and the Holocaust* (Syracuse University Press, 2005)

Hirsch, Marianne, *Family Frames: Photography, Narrative and Postmemory* (Harvard University Press, 2012)

Hirsch, Marianne, *The Generation of Postmemory: Writing and Visual Culture After the Holocaust* (Columbia University Press, 2012)

Hoffman, Eva, *After Such Knowledge: A Meditation on the Aftermath of the Holocaust* (Secker & Warburg, 2003)

Hoffmann-Curtius, Kathrin, *Bilder zum Judenmord* (Jonas Verlag F. Kunst U., 2014), translated as *Judenmord: Art and the Holocaust in Post-war Germany* (Reaktion Books, 2018)

Raczymow, Henri, *Contes d'exil et d'oubli* (Gallimard, 1979) (two extracts have appeared in English: in *Yale French Studies*, no 85, transl. Alan Astro; and on the website jewishfiction.net, transl. Robert Bononno, October 2013)

Rothberg, Michael, *Multidirectional Memory: Remembering the Holocaust in the Age of Decolonization* (Stanford University Press, 2009)

Rubin Suleiman, Susan, 'Monuments in a foreign tongue: on reading Holocaust memoirs by emigrants', in Susan Rubin Suleiman (ed.), *Exile and Creativity: Signposts, Travelers, Outsiders, Backward Glances* (Duke University Press, 1998)

Wardi, Dina, *Memorial Candles: Children of the Holocaust* (Routledge, 1992)

Artist websites and texts (in the order they appear in the text):

Ardyn Halter, www.ardynhalter.com/home

Halter, Ardyn, *The Fire and the Bonfire* (Second Generation Publishing, forthcoming)

Julie Held, www.julieheld.com/

Susie Mendelsson, https://susiemendelsson.co.uk/

Marlene Rolfe, https://artuk.org/discover/artists/rolfe-marlene-b-1946

Barbara Loftus, www.barbaraloftus.co.uk/

Ruth Rix, www.ruthrix.com/

Judith Tucker, www.judithtuckerartist.com/

Tucker, J., 'The Lido in the Forest: Painting, Memory and Subjectivity', in Elizabeth Anderson, Avril Maddrell, Kate McLoughlin and Alana Vincent (eds.), *Memory, Mourning and Landscape: Interdisciplinary Essays* (Rodopi Press, 2012)

Tucker, J., 'Brooding on Bornholm: Postmemory, Painting and Place' in Owain Jones and Joanne Garde-Hansen (eds.), *Geography and Memory* (Palgrave Macmillan, 2012)

Sara Davidmann, www.saradavidmann.com/

Davidmann, Sara, *Mischling 1* (Gost Books, 2021)

Lily Markiewicz, https://land2.leeds.ac.uk/people/markiewicz/, www.leeds.ac.uk/cath/ahrc/events/2004/1105/abs/markiewicz.html

Julia Winckler, www.juliawinckler.com/

Lorna Brunstein, https://lornabrunstein.wordpress.com/

Yishay Garbasz, http://yishay.com/, www.versobooks.com/blogs/2463-in-my-mother-s-footsteps-by-yishay-garbasz

Jen Kagan, https://jenkagan.com

Jenny Stolzenberg, www.theguardian.com/artanddesign/2016/sep/13/jenny-stolzenberg-obituary, https://colinshindler.com/remembering-jenny-stolzenberg/

Monica Petzal, https://monicapetzal.com/

Natasha Kerr, http://collections.vam.ac.uk/item/O154238/at-the-end-of-the-hanging-kerr-natasha/

Julia Burton and Rosalind Gelbart ('45 Aid Society), https://45aid.org/memory-quilt/

Gideon Summerfield, www. gideonsummerfield.com

Films

Julie Held: *Inside the Outside*
Barbara Loftus: *Carrying the Candle*
Ruth Rix: *The Precipice Behind*

These short films were filmed and edited in 2019 by Andrew Snell with Eileen Hughes for Insiders/Outsiders. Visit https://insidersoutsidersfestival.org/ for more information and video links.

FROM THE *JR* ARCHIVE

'DIASPORISM IN ART', BY DIANA POPESCU

In this article from July 2011's issue of JR, *Diana Popescu explored how young Israeli artists were becoming political activists – with the aim of returning to a European homeland.*

Diana Popescu is Associate Research Fellow at Pears Institute for the Study of Antisemitism, Birkbeck College, and editor of Genocide Studies and Prevention: An International Journal (GSP). *Her research and teaching include Holocaust studies, art history and museum studies. She has published work on the ethics and aesthetics of Holocaust representation in museums and in the visual arts.*

A community of artists from Israel who came of age in the 1990s are seeking alternatives to the Zionist dream – in lands away from Israel. Their new ideology, given the name Retro Zionism by artist Yael Bartana, encourages us to look backwards to the lands of destruction that were left behind in Europe.

Europe, though 'repressed' from the Israeli collective psyche, has paradoxically remained a part of it, weighing upon its present. It surfaces in the Holocaust survivors' testimonies about the demonic 'world of over-there' or in the memories imbued with nostalgia of the Jewish pioneers in Israel. 'New historians' have coined the phrase 'shlilat shlilat ha-galut', which translates as 'the negation of the negation of exile'. Diasporism is another term used as an acknowledgement of diaspora as a positive phase in Jewish existence and as a 'legitimate' component of the Israeli collective self.

This emerged in post-Holocaust literary culture and in the visual arts. Self-exiled American Jew in London, artist R.B. Kitaj, in his *First Diasporist Manifesto* (1989), observed that 'galut (exile) had become a way of life and death, consonant with Jewishness itself, even though Israel is reborn'.

Artists too are now assuming the role of critical storytellers of the Jewish saga in Israel, challenging the notion that Jewish homeland can happen in Israel only and proposing 'Europeanism' as an alternative to the Jewish condition in Israel.

Their artworks aim to transcend the boundaries of art and become manifestos of real political movements.

Mary Koszmary (Nightmares), made in 2007 by Yael Bartana (b. 1970), is a video-work and part of a larger project titled *Polish Trilogy*. Her protagonist, Slawomir Sierakowski, is in real life a left-wing political critic and activist in Poland. We see him as he emerges from a dark tunnel and enters Warsaw's now dilapidated and empty Olympic Stadium – a vast amphitheatre which, for decades, served as a venue for sporting events and state ceremonies. There he stops to deliver an impassioned speech, in which he calls the three million Jews to return to their homeland, Poland, and chase away its demons.

'Today we are fed up looking at our similar faces. On the streets of our great cities, we are on the lookout for strangers and listening intently when they speak. Yes! Today we know that we cannot live alone. We need the other, and there's no closer other for us than you. Return!'

As he speaks, children in school uniforms stencil on the green field the key message of Sierakowski's speech: 'Three million Jews can change the lives of 40 million Poles.' Sierakowski's grave demeanour and powerful echoing voice has the effect of awakening a Jewish longing for a European homeland, long suppressed in the Israeli consciousness, as it was often coupled with a feeling of collective pain induced by the brutal separation of Jews from Europe. Nostalgia – the core emotion conveyed in *Mary Koszmary* – should not be seen as a gratuitous Jewish reminiscence over an impossible return, argues Bartana. She asks her viewers to adopt an alternative mode of thinking which can alter reality, and by means of which the Jewish return to Europe is not utopian but feasible.

In the second video-work of the Polish trilogy, *Wall and Tower* (2009), Bartana shows us that nostalgia can indeed lead to activism. The film records how a group of young Israeli and Polish volunteers, dressed as the Jewish immigrants to Palestine in the 1930s, enact Sierakowski's call and, following the model of Israel's first kibbutz, Hum ve-Migdal, they build Europe's first kibbutz, situated on the site of the Warsaw Ghetto Uprising.

This is a symbolic 'displacement' as the historic kibbutz, marking the beginnings of the Zionist enterprise, is dislodged to Europe. The film's most dominant images are those gestures of Jewish-Polish reunion, such as the engraving of the Jewish-Polish flag on the wooden walls of the kibbutz.

Bartana deliberately blurs the lines separating myth and fact and creates a sense of doubt and ambivalence as she informs her audience that her real intention is to establish, together with Sierakowski, a Jewish Renaissance Movement in Poland. Charged with multinational symbolism, the movement includes a flag with a coat of arms merging the Polish eagle and the Jewish Star of David, marking the beginning of a new Polish-Jewish symbiosis, a 'hybrid that embodies both a traumatic history and the Zionist dream'. She proposes that the movement is accompanied by a congress reminiscent of the First Zionist Congress. *Wall and Tower* reaffirms Bartana's aim as an artist – that is, to interrogate and challenge fixed ideas even at risk of moving away from art: 'What is of interest to me is to stimulate real reflection, even at the price of moving away from the sphere of art … I am seriously interested in forming a real political party.'

Artist and journalist Ronen Eidelman's art project, *Medinat Weimar*, similarly borders on political activism. Despite initial doubts as to whether Bartana's project could bring anything new, Eidelman decided 'to take the idea to the streets and test it there'. His art project comprises thirteen principles establishing the foundation of a Jewish State in Thuringia, a state in the east of Germany, home to Weimar.

Using language reminiscent of Herzl's Zionism, the Jewish State in Thuringia is described as a 'resolution to the plight of world Jewry', an expression of people's right of 'self-redetermination and self-redefinition' and a 'peaceful home addressing the failure of the Zionist claim to "normalise" the Jewish people and establish a safe haven'.

Eidelman's project was taken into the streets of Weimar in June 2008, starting with a rally and conference organised to celebrate its establishment. Banners, symbols, flags and songs made up the setting of a carefully orchestrated demonstration. The project attracted media attention and a public discussion about the possibility of a 'second Israel'. It also brought together other 'diasporist' voices emerging on the art scene, such as Amit Epstein, an Israeli artist living in Berlin. Epstein's project 'Bundesland Israel', strikingly similar to Eidelman's, promoted the establishment of an 'Israel away from Israel'. Due to lack of funding, however, this project was never shown to the public. His latest work is the video trilogy *The Stockholm Syndrome* where a complicated, victim-victimiser dynamic is informed by the rise, fall, and notional revenge of European Jewry.

When collective forms of thinking are created and many of the same ideas surface in different places, one can argue that this is an expression of zeitgeist, the mood and socio-cultural direction taken by a new generation. Israeli cultural life is witnessing a flourishing of Jewish 'alternative histories' of return to diaspora. In Dudu Busi's novel *Mother is Longing for Words* (2006), the main character, a Mizrahi Jew and former paratrooper officer in the Lebanon War, moves to Germany to start anew. Michael Blum's art project *Exodus 2048* is an apocalyptic representation of Israel in 2048 defeated by its Pakistani and Iranian enemies, having lost US support. Blum recreates the situation of the 'wandering Jew', telling the story of a group of Israeli refugees stranded on a Maltese ferry, roaming in the North Sea near Rotterdam.

Statistics confirm that more and more Israelis perceive Europe as a second home. In 2005, the Ministry of Immigrant Absorption announced that approximately 750,000 Israelis were living abroad, of whom 25 per cent were in Europe. More than 4,000 Israelis received German citizenship in 2007, which suggests a 50 per cent increase over 2005 – the largest number in twenty-five years. According to German authorities there are more than 4,000 Israelis registered as living in Berlin alone. Some estimate that the figure could be as high as 15,000.

Artist Amit Epstein, for example, sees himself as one of the 'returnees to the world that spewed out his family during the war'. Epstein is a frequent contributor to *Eretz Acheret* (A Different Country) – an online journal supporting the concept of diasporism.

In his 2009 article *La Deutsche Vita* (a reference to Fellini's *La Dolce Vita* – sweet/good life) Epstein tells of the 'new wave of Israeli immigration to Berlin', suggesting that to them Berlin feels like 'home'.

Diasporism thus appears as a real phenomenon among Israel's young generation. An article in the *Jerusalem Post* significantly titled 'The Demise of Ideology' describes the changes in the Israeli perception of immigration. Those who leave are no longer perceived by Israeli society as 'yordim', a term used to refer to deserters or traitors, but simply as 'Israelis living abroad'. 'There is no longer any badge of shame for yordim', says Prof Oz Almog, a sociologist at Haifa University. 'On the contrary, in the era of globalisation, success means international success. So an Israeli who makes it big abroad is not 'going down' but 'going up' in prestige.'

The recent waves of Israeli immigration to European countries confirm that 'return' is indeed feasible. This bestows a degree of legitimacy on the artists' projects, showing how common it is for art to mirror history and become a conveyer of 'the spirit of the times'. Artists are often deemed thinkers ahead of their times, foreseers of what is to come. Their role is to advance ideas, thoughts and beliefs that are already permeating society and which can later turn into facts.

Theodor Herzl, an artist himself, was able to register the 'pulse' of his times and challenge conceptions or mental constructs that framed Jewish thought. His radical vision was seen by his contemporaries as more ludicrous than sensible. Subsequently, history has shown that Zionism can turn diaspora into a mere alternative to Jewish life. On its 63rd anniversary, the Jewish homeland has become a 'choice' rather than an imperative, as Europe is increasingly present not only in the Israeli consciousness but also in the concrete lives of many Israelis.

Auschwitz–Birkenau (from Traces series) by Julia Winckler, photographic image (made using analogue medium format film), 1189 x 841mm, 2001. (Photo: Julia Winckler)

After Auschwitz installation (detail) by Lorna Brunstein at the Hundred Years Gallery, London, multimedia installation featuring floor and wall pieces, video projection and soundscape, September 2019. (Photo: Lorna Brunstein)

Video still from the performance *The Number Project* by Yishay Garbasz, HD video, run time 4 min, 2011. (Courtesy of the artist and Ronald Feldman Gallery)

Interactive Suitcase - The First Date by Jenny Kagan, reclaimed suitcase, fabric, string, pulleys, projector, reed switch, sound player, speaker, 900 x 550mm, 2016. (Photo: Jenny Kagan)

Dissent and Displacement, Panel 6C by Monica Petzal, lithograph over monoprint, 100 x 70cm, 2020 (Photo: Justin Piperger)

Bridge Party by Barbara Loftus, oil on canvas, 81 x 114cm, 2010. (Photo: Bernard G. Mills)

Holocaust Survivor Lily Ebert, from *Legacy of Survival* project by Gideon Summerfield, pencil, acrylic and pastel on paper, 42 x 59.4cm, 2018. (Gideon Summerfield)

Munich, 2006, directed by Steven Spielberg, with Eric Bana (left) and Geoffrey Rush. (Collection Christophel / Alamy Stock Photo)

The Pianist, 2002, directed by Roman Polanski, with Adrien Brody. (United Archives GmbH / Alamy Stock Photo)

The Reader, 2008, directed by Stephen Daldry. (Allstar Picture Library Ltd / Alamy Stock Photo)

The Boy in the Striped Pyjamas, 2008, directed by Mark Herman, with Jack Scanlon and Asa Butterfield. (AF archive / Alamy Stock Photo)

Jojo Rabbit, 2018, directed by Taika Waititi, with, from left: Roman Griffin Davis, Taika Waititi and Scarlett Johansson. (Pictorial Press Ltd / Alamy Stock Photo)

Wonder Woman, 2017, directed by Patty Jenkins, with Gal Gadot. (Pictorial Press Ltd / Alamy Stock Photo)

Denial, 2016, directed by Mick Jackson, with Timothy Spall. (AF archive / Alamy Stock Photo)

Borat: Cultural Learnings Of America For Make Benefit Glorious Nation Of Kazakhstan, 2006, directed by Larry Charles, with Sacha Baron Cohen. (AA Film Archive / Alamy Stock Photo)

FROM THE *JR* ARCHIVE

'A TALE OF TWO CITIES', BY MONICA PETZAL

Dresden and Coventry have long been united by the terrible legacy of Second World War bombing. In this piece from January 2016, artist Monica Petzal revealed how her own family history links her to both cities and led to the development of her art series, The Dresden Project.

Monica Petzal is an artist, art historian, critic and curator. Her work can be found in public collections including the V&A Museum, London and New Hall College Art Collection, University of Cambridge.

Growing up in the 1950s and 60s at the edge of Hampstead Heath, I did not think that I was mostly German; indeed, I was determinedly British. Throughout their lives, my parents, German Jewish refugees, sustained the language, culture, and lifestyle of their native Berlin and Dresden. Religion did not figure. However, in their own peculiar way they felt assimilated and were deeply attached and loyal to the country that had given them refuge.

My father, his study shelves lined with the books of testimony from the Nuremberg Trials and Winston Churchill's history of Second World War, never spoke of his immediate family, all of whom had died in Auschwitz. My mother, however, spoke glowingly of Dresden, its beauty and culture, and our house was full of Dresden porcelain and German silver.

As an artist, I chose to put my complex heritage mostly to one side, until I realised the narratives were emerging without my conscious consent. As I approached my 60th birthday, I decided I had to confront this and in July 2012 went on reconnaissance to Dresden. Welcomed at the Grafikwerkstatt, a remarkable, city-owned print workshop, I eventually worked there for two lengthy periods in 2013 and 2014.

The Dresden Project which emerged explores my extensive family archive, historical documentation, and personal experience through the medium of print, also considering the Allied bombing of Dresden in February 1945, its aftermath and some aspects of contemporary cultural and political life in Dresden.

My mother, Hannalore (Lore) Isakowitz, was born in 1915, and her parents Erich Max Isakowitz, a dental surgeon, and Sofie Berlowitz came to Dresden in the early 1920s to escape growing antisemitism in their native eastern Prussia. They became active members of the cultured Jewish bourgeoisie, including amongst their friends the expressionist painter Conrad Felixmüller and the academic and diarist Victor Klemperer. From the late 1920s they lived in Dresden Plauen; Lore went to the Deutsche Oberschule in Plauen, receiving her Abitur in spring 1933. From then on daily life became increasingly constrained; Lore, a student of Klemperer, was not allowed to attend university, and Erich was not allowed to treat Aryans.

Sofie travelled to London in 1935, and petitioned successfully for permission for Erich to work in London, accompanied by his family. In his famous diaries, *I Shall Bear Witness*, Klemperer gives a revealing account of my grandparents' and mother's last years in Dresden and their eventual departure. Erich and Sofie settled in Hampstead in the summer of 1936, and were never to see Germany again. Lore married and had three children, my two older brothers and me. Our family visited Dresden in 1985, then still a city of the DDR and largely in ruins. For Lore it was a traumatic visit in every way; highly distressed, she never recovered her equilibrium, and died the following year.

My mother and her family had fled the Nazis in a relatively well-planned way – their ability to leave due to foresight and financial means. By contrast, my father Harry Petzal, born in Berlin in 1908, escaped just before war broke out on forged papers. He requested asylum and volunteered for the military. Not interned because of his specialism as a metallurgist, he served in the British Army Pioneer Corps, and from 1943 at Lucas, which made aircraft components. His expertise may have contributed in some small measure to the allied bombing.

Both sides of my family had considered themselves 'more German than the Germans', both grandfathers fought for Germany in the First World War, one winning the Iron Cross. The fortunate ones who fled were devastated at being forced to leave their homeland. Britain did not welcome them warmly, but it did take them in. The German Jewish refugee community flourished and the immense contribution Hitler's émigrés made to British life and culture is widely recognised – their narrative is as relevant today as it was then.

Initially a personal exploration, I could not have foreseen that my project would be exhibited at the Kreuzkirche in the heart of Dresden as a significant part of the 75th commemoration of the bombing. Nor did I contemplate the thought that it would lead me to reclaim my German citizenship, join the board of the reconciliation charity the Dresden Trust, and accept the challenge to produce artwork for Coventry.

75/70 is a site-specific installation for Coventry Cathedral to commemorate the 75th anniversary of the bombing of the city by the German Luftwaffe on 14 November 1940. A series of twenty prints, in four 'towers', it concerns the twinned cities of Coventry and Dresden and the wider destruction of the cities of Britain and Germany during Second World War. Conceived to reflect the scale and significance of the cathedral, it addresses the historical background of the cities: the bombing and destruction; reconstruction; and contemporary life in both places.

Flanking the printed images, with the names of Coventry and Dresden uppermost, are the place names of the thirty-two other most bombed towns and cities in Great Britain and Germany during Second World War.

While I am now involved with Coventry, exhibiting 75/70 in the Cathedral and the Dresden Project at the Herbert Art Gallery & Museum, the city has none of the tragedy I associate with my relationship to Dresden, which remains a highly politicised and fragmented city permeated by a culture of remembrance.

Making this artwork has altered my connection to my heritage. I am more politicised and have a greater awareness of German history and current events, in particular the rise of the anti-Islam movement Pegida in Dresden. As someone who now holds dual British and German nationality, and as a Jew, I want my work to emphasise the significance of individual stories, as well as the importance of reconciliation between countries and faiths. The Dresden Project is about us all. It asks us to consider how we construct our own histories and how we understand who we are and what we stand for.

IN BEAUTY AND IN UGLINESS: HOW JEWISH FILMMAKERS ARE BREAKING DOWN THE STEREOTYPES

NATHAN ABRAMS

Until recently, Jewish filmmakers have been defensive. They have taken the attitude that it is better to focus on the 'good' side of being Jewish. The mentality has been 'let us only show our clean laundry to the goyim (non-Jews)'. Given that for most of the twentieth century Jews have been subjected to both overt and covert antisemitism this is hardly surprising. By contrast, over the last two decades, there has been a clear change in how Jewish filmmakers depict Jews and how Jews are portrayed on film in general. The impetus to be apologetic has disappeared, to be replaced by one that is more open, self-critical and playful, and which presents Jews warts and all to the world, in beauty and ugliness, as well as Jews appearing in places and spaces least expected. It is a vision that shows Jews are more comfortable with their place in the world, that they are moving beyond the stereotypes of the past into new and exciting territory.

In this respect, a good place to begin is with the image of Israel. For years, the image that has most often been used outside of Israel to represent the country in film is the iconic image of the suave and sophisticated Israeli spy. Mossad, Israel's secret intelligence service, has a reputation for being fearsomely effective, protecting Israelis at home and Jews far beyond the country's borders. Films such as *The House on Garibaldi Street* (1979) or *Operation Finale* (2018) play up Mossad's success in their depictions of the capture of top Nazi bureaucrat Adolf

Eichmann. *Operation Thunderbolt* (1977), *Raid on Entebbe* (1977) and *Entebbe* (2018) replay the Israeli rescue of hijacked hostages from Uganda.

But the fearsome myth of Mossad has been dented lately. Recent films portray Mossad secret agents with tarnished reputations and frequently ineffective in their missions. These depictions are tied up with the rise of Keshet, the phenomenally successful Israeli TV company that has been behind some of the most popular TV dramas globally over the past decade, including Hebrew-language originals such as *Prisoners of War* (2010) and its American remake, *Homeland* (2011) (featuring the Jewish CIA operator Saul Berenson played by Mandy Patinkin). Other productions, including *Hostages* (originally made in Hebrew for Channel 10 and then remade by CBS in 2013), *Mossad 101* (a 2015 Israeli series), and two original Netflix series, *The Spy* (2019), and *Fauda* (2015) also take a more clear-eyed view of Israel's secret services, showing them in a relatively negative light. These films show a vulnerability and break down in a traditional stereotype that often depicts Israeli machismo. In these films we see Israel as just another country trying to defend itself.

As American Jews begin to question Israel's policies and become more disillusioned with the continued occupation and the policies of the Netanyahu government, filmmakers in the diaspora are similarly challenging the traditional stereotype of Israel on film. David Mamet's 1991 police procedural, *Homicide*, foregrounded this trend, with its portrayal of Israeli secret agents blackmailing and double-crossing an American Jewish police officer and taking advantage of his help.

Israel's failure to always be able to protect its citizens abroad is vividly portrayed in Steven Spielberg's *Munich* (2005), which begins and ends with images of the capture and killing of the eleven Israeli athletes at the 1972 Olympic Games. The counter-assassination team assigned to kill the leaders of Black September, the Palestinian organisation responsible for the massacre, are portrayed as bumbling and clumsy. They just do not live up to Mossad's global reputation. Mistakes, blunders and errors recur throughout the film. The team are unduly reliant on a shadowy French outfit for their logistics, weapons, intelligence and safe houses. This leads to one mix-up when the Israelis and Palestinians share a room for the night. Three of the original five-member squad are killed. The team is ineffectual against the hydra-like rise of terror and, by the end of the film, its leader Avner (Eric Bana) becomes an obsessive paranoid. Convinced that Mossad wants him dead, he rejects Israel and abandons his homeland for the United States, permanently moving his family to Brooklyn – as if to say that this part of the diaspora is the safest haven for Jews.

Another reason that it is not a gung-ho celebratory affair is that the film reflects on the efficacy of targeted assassinations as practised by the United States and

Israel during the so-called War on Terror, the military campaign launched by the US and its allies after 11 September 2001. Written with Tony Kushner and Eric Roth, *Munich* explores the counter-productivity of counter-terrorism, drawing on the response of the Israeli government to the 1972 Munich massacre to make points about Israeli and American policy in the twenty-first century. The tone of the film becomes darker as it progresses: the lead character is a chef and Spielberg equates being a butcher with butchery, as if the activities of the Mossad team are not kosher. Notably many of the leads (famous French film director Matthieu Kassovitz aside) are not played by Jewish actors.

Israeli films are even harsher in their depictions of their secret service. In *Walk on Water* (2004), Mossad operative Eyal (Lior Ashkenazi) transforms from tough guy to impotent bystander during the film. In the opening sequences we see him effortlessly assassinate a Hamas leader by injecting him with poison. By the end, paralysed by doubt, he is unable to kill an elderly Nazi war criminal. As if to compound his indecision, the killing is finally carried out by the Nazi's gay grandson. In *The Debt* (2010) – a British remake of the Israeli *Ha-Hov* (2007) – three young Mossad agents are sent on a secret mission to capture and kill a notorious Nazi war criminal. When, thirty years later, a man claiming to be that Nazi surfaces in Ukraine, it is revealed that not only did they fail in their original mission (the Nazi escapes and permanently scars the hero) but also that they covered up their failure for three decades.

Such films also poke fun at the image of the tough Israeli spy. In *You Don't Mess with the Zohan* (2008), a former Israeli Defence Forces (IDF) counter-terrorist, Zohan Dvir, wants to give up fighting and become a hairdresser. He moves to New York and reinvents himself with hilarious consequences, until his old life catches up with him. At the same time, as with the character of Avner in *Munich*, these agents are still presented as sympathetic, and often attractive protagonists.

But these images impugn the once-sacrosanct notion of Israeli efficiency and suggest that the Israeli spy, as embodied by the Mossad agent, is not as one-dimensionally tough as presented in the past. So, there is no doubt that Israel, and specifically the Israeli secret service, is suffering on screen. No James Bond or Jack Bauer here. It is only in recent years that we have seen deep divisions open among Jews across the world, and a decreasing sense of identification with Israel. As these trends deepen, and we see a potentially greater fragmenting of views within the diaspora, and beyond, it will be interesting to see what happens next to the Mossad agent on screen.

The trend towards self-criticism and openness has led to some remarkable documentaries both by Jews and about Jewish subjects. *Trembling Before G-d* by Sandi Simcha Dubowski (2001) explored the topic of homosexuality in the

Jewish Orthodox world, Hasidic and otherwise. Documentaries shedding light on Jewish criminal and deviant sexual behaviour have also appeared. *Crazy Love*, directed by Dan Klores and Fisher Stevens in 2007, explores the relationship between Burt Pugach and his much younger girlfriend and wife, Linda Riss. Pugach, a lawyer, served fourteen years in prison for hiring men to blind and scar her with lye when she tried to break up with him. *Capturing the Friedmans* (2003) traces the investigation of Arnold Friedman and his son Jesse for child molestation. *Rewind* (2019) by Sasha Joseph Neulinger looks at multigenerational sex abuse by a famous New York cantor from the perspective of one of his victims. There has been at least one Netflix documentary about Jeffrey Epstein and Harvey Weinstein respectively, and no doubt there will be more.

As these above documentaries show, recent cinema has not shied away from exploring the uglier sides of Jewishness. *Mank* (2020), David Fincher's biopic of Herman J. Mankewiecz, who wrote the classic 1941 film *Citizen Kane*, depicts the eponymous protagonist as a washed-up boozer (albeit with a conscience). Real-life movie mogul Louis B. Mayer is depicted as a mean-spirited, money-grubbing right-winger whose concern is less for the underdog and the poor than with keeping profits in the face of the Depression.

Fictional films send up such characters. These build upon the Coen brothers' wonderful *Barton Fink* (1991) in which Michael Lerner sends up Mayer (among other moguls) in his portrait of a fictional Capitol studio boss, Jack Lipnick. In *Tropic Thunder* (2008), Tom Cruise plays Les Grossman, a profane, heavy-pawed, hirsute but balding exaggeration of Jewish producers such as Scott Rudin and Joel Silver, who cares more for money than human life. Some might complain the depiction is antisemitic, but in the hands of the Israeli-American screen-writer Etan Cohen and director Ben Stiller, it reads more like a caricature of an antisemitic stereotype, showing how modern Jewish cinema is not afraid to laugh at itself.

Jordan Belfort (Leonard DiCaprio) in *The Wolf of Wall Street* (2013) is a lying, dishonest, coke-snorting, philandering trader. Although his ethnicity and religion are played down – or even whitewashed by having DiCaprio play him – we know that Belfort is supposed to be Jewish: Jewish director Rob Reiner plays his father, Max, and Belfort is surrounded by an entourage of explicitly Jewish friends and family, many of whom indulge in the same behaviour as Belfort.

Capping these representations is Adam Sandler's character, Howard Ratner, in 2019's *Uncut Gems*. He is morally, ethically and physically ugly – imagine the unholy offspring of a marriage between Sacha Baron Cohen and Al Pacino – and subjected to an endless Wurlitzer of dealing, pawning and gambling. He is a low-class Bernie Madoff, building a crumbling empire on a Ponzi scheme.

To throw in a British analogy, he is a latter-day Del Boy who you can imagine saying, 'This time next year, we'll be *millionaires*'. Howard – can you get a name trying to hide more Judaism than that? – plays a jeweller just like his namesake, the British jeweller Gerald Ratner (who famously described some of his products as 'total crap'). Such an expression describes much of what Howard sells in his store, namely vulgar *tchatckes* (trinkets). Howard is a *shpritzer,* shooting his mouth off incessantly, talking himself into and out of trouble. His monologues are interspersed with Yiddish and profanities (there were so many 'fucks' that my mum walked out of the film).

★★★

Even when it comes to what one may consider the most sacrosanct element of Jewish cinema, the Holocaust, films have become more nuanced. Between 1989 and 2003, over 170 new Holocaust films were made. If one were to expand the list to those films that included the Holocaust as a secondary plotline, the figure balloons to 400. A qualitative change has taken place alongside this quantitative shift. In contrast to earlier decades, many of these films incorporated provocative material. In mainstream US cinema the Holocaust has even been conceived of as material for humour. Contemporary cinema is also beginning to present a new paradigm in Holocaust filmmaking in its refusal to only present uncomplicated representation of Jews as weak, passive and undeserving victims, asking questions that may have been considered taboo during the preceding seventy-five years. Furthermore, there are those films in which the Holocaust is made inexplicit, but tangible, through their use of imagery, cinematography, iconography and themes, but which space prevents me from exploring in further depth. Science-fiction films have proved particularly in their use of Holocaust parallels, metaphors and analogies. Where it might be argued that a post-Holocaust sensibility informs all Jewish filmmaking after 1945, there have certainly been some remarkable films dealing with the Holocaust during this period.

Recent cinema complicates the boundary between Jewish victimhood and Nazi guilt. As its title implies, *The Grey Zone* (2001), directed by Tim Blake Nelson explores that ambiguous 'grey zone' in which the sharp distinctions between Nazi perpetrators and their victims are blurred. *The Grey Zone*, which is based on real events, focuses on the role of the Sonderkommando (Special Commando), those concentration camp inmates selected by the SS to aid with the killing process, and asks some tough questions about the distinction between victim and victimiser. The striking Hungarian-made *Son of Saul* (2015) depicts a similar theme in what is probably the most harrowing Holocaust film ever made. *Son of Saul* put us directly among the Sonderkommando in a way never seen before. Ingeniously shot, it both hinted at and showed the horror of the Nazis' industrialised murder machine, eased with ghastly efficiency by the Jews forced to run it.

Roman Polanski's historically based film *The Pianist* (2002) similarly refuses to idealise Jews as victims. Roman Polanski built upon his 'apartment trilogy' – *Repulsion* (1965), *Rosemary's Baby* (1968) and *The Tenant* (1976) – which only hinted at his wartime experiences through allegories of trapped women (mainly) menaced by unseen forces, to depict the remarkable story of the pianist Wladislaw Spielmann. Holocaust imagery also found its way into his remake of the classic Charles Dickens story *Oliver Twist* (2005), which makes consistent visual reference to the Holocaust in attempting to depict the horror of Oliver's existence, paralleling Polanski's own childhood in wartime Poland. This is particularly established in the opening sequence, where the children in the orphanage are all dressed in matching shabby uniforms and look up at Oliver with glassy eyes. In the children's empty, hollow stares, it's difficult not to see echoes of 'pyjama' clad concentration camp inmates.

However, *The Pianist* was the first movie in which Polanski confronted the horror he had directly experienced. Several British films also blur the distinction between victim and victimiser during the Holocaust. *The Reader* (2008), directed by Stephen Daldry, focuses on the illiterate former SS guard Hanna Schmitz (played by Kate Winslet), an ageing woman who is abandoned, isolated and dirty and on the verge of killing herself in prison. As the film progresses, one almost feels sorry for the impoverished guard when contrasted to the wealthy Holocaust survivor, Ilana, who refuses the money that Hanna leaves to her after she commits suicide in prison.

The Boy in the Striped Pyjamas (2008) directed by Mark Herman, follows an 8-year-old German boy whose father is the commandant of an unnamed concentration camp and who befriends a Jewish inmate. The film was controversial because of its blurring of the identities of Jew and Nazi, both of whom suffer the same fate, leaving us focused not on the Jewish victims but the despairing parents of the missing German child whose fate they begin to suspect.

Like *The Boy in the Striped Pyjamas*, the 2019 film *Jojo Rabbit* presents the Holocaust from the perspective of a German child. The eponymous character, played by Roman Griffin Davis, is Johannes 'Jojo' Betzler, a 10-year-old who is on the cusp of joining the Hitler Youth. He is a fanatical Nazi. As he says, 'I'm massively into swastikas.' He is so avid that not only does he have an imaginary friend, but that that friend is Hitler (albeit played by the Jewish and Maori director Taika Waititi). Jojo's Nazi beliefs are further tested when he discovers that his mother Rosie (Scarlett Johansson) is hiding a Jewish girl (Thomasin McKenzie) in their attic. A friendship forms between them and the film gradually shifts, giving a Jewish child's perspective on the war and ridiculing Nazi stereotypes of Jews.

With a cast that includes Sam Rockwell, Rebel Wilson and Stephen Merchant *Jojo Rabbit* has more in common with Mel Brooks' legendary and prophetic 1968 film *The Producers* (which saw a remake in 2005) and with elements of Quentin Tarantino's *Inglourious Basterds* (2009) than it does with the more serious *Boy in the Striped Pyjamas*. The non-standard nature of this Holocaust film is reinforced not only by its comedy but also by its cinematic style.

Waititi presents a postcard-pretty picture box German town (in reality, it is in the Czech Republic) against a soundtrack that opens with the Beatles' 'I Want to Hold Your Hand' and closes with David Bowie's 'Heroes' (both sung in German). The film also features the Bowie track 'Cat People' (with its lyric 'putting out fire with gasoline') - a nod to Tarantino, who uses the same song in *Inglourious Basterds*.

The Holocaust is also permeating genres that are not about the Holocaust. Since making *Schindler's List* in 1993, Steven Spielberg seems to have become more comfortable in his own skin and many of the films he has directed since then hold references to Jewish themes and tropes. His *A.I. Artificial Intelligence* (2001), *War of the Worlds* (2005) and even *The BFG* (2016) can be analysed from a Holocaust perspective if you look closely enough. Indiana Jones (played by the Jewish Harrison Ford) explodes the myth of the bookish professorial Jew who is always battling Nazis; as he says in *The Last Crusade* (1989), 'Nazis, I hate these guys.' The mutant Magneto (played by Ian McKellen and later Michael Fassbender) in the superhero *X-Men* films is a key exception: he is explicitly marked as a Jewish Holocaust survivor.

In the Harry Potter films, based on J.K. Rowling's children's books, Harry opposes a fascistic death-worshipping cult, led by a dictatorial ruler, who wishes to cleanse his race of any impurities. His followers use the racialist, eugenicist language of the Nazis. They inflict death and suffering. As Jenny Singer wrote in *The Forward*, 'Rowling's books borrow tremendously from the experience of Jews and other targeted groups in the Holocaust.' This metaphor has been acknowledged by plenty of others who have recognised traces of the Second World War in the franchise: the evil wizard Lord Voldemort in the films embodies slavery in Egypt, the Spanish Inquisition and the Holocaust rolled into one. However, there is one problematic representation in the books and film: the goblins of Gringotts. These bankers – a profession historically associated with Jews – are hooked-nosed and swarthy, obsessed with gold and secrecy. They have been criticised for replicating anti-Jewish tropes.

Although the British director Ridley Scott is not Jewish, he liberally peppered his 2014 film *Exodus: Of Gods and Kings*, with references to the Shoah. The Egyptians are presented as Nazis, hanging innocent men, women and children to flush out Moses, who is hiding among them. The Hebrew slaves are shown concealed in cellars to escape an Egyptian *Aktion*. Pithom becomes the Warsaw Ghetto and Moses is transformed into the Warsaw Ghetto Rising leader Mordechai Anielewicz.

Understandably, the one genre where one can find most allusions to the Holocaust, albeit often oblique, is Jewish horror, which surely characterises the Jewish experience in the diaspora for much of two millennia but especially in the second half of the twentieth century. Jewish directors have been prominent in the genre, making some of its most memorable films: from Curt and Robert Siodmak, Roger Corman and Edgar Ulmer, to the 'new horror' of the 1960s created by directors such as Roman Polanski, Stanley Kubrick, William Friedkin, Richard Donner and Steven Spielberg (and also parodied by Mel Brooks). They transformed the horror genre from one of vampires, werewolves and other semi-human monsters into one in which evil has become more metaphysical and perpetrated by humans. On the surface, there is nothing obviously Jewish about them but scratch a little deeper and we can see that their worldview is motivated by the Jewish experience of the Holocaust and its aftermath. Consider how the Holocaust influenced Alfred Hitchcock's *Psycho* (1960), which in turn exercised a strong formalistic influence on *Schindler's List*. Hitchcock was asked to edit documentary footage from the camps and the memory of this arguably seeped into *Psycho* with its use of a modern setting – especially the bright, clean shower – as a site of a savage murder.

Following in their wake, the Jewish horror directors of the twenty-first century are also channelling a Jewish worldview. In Eli Roth's work – *Cabin Fever* (2002), *Hostel* (2005) and *Hostel: Part II* (2007) – echoes of the Holocaust can be found not least in their gore, which has been labelled 'torture porn' or 'gorno' – although the sedimented effects of the War on Terror also play a part here.

The Unborn (2009), directed by David S Goyer, blended horror with the Holocaust, and in 2012 Sam Raimi (who also directed *Evil Dead*) produced another *dybbuk* film (Yiddish word for an evil spirit or demon that has a human form) in *The Possession*, a rehash of *The Exorcist* and *Poltergeist* but with a Jewish twist. Another *dybbuk* appeared in 2019's *The Vigil*, another film steeped in Jewish lore, this time as an ex-Hasidic Jewish man agrees to be the *shomer* of the body of a deceased person (in accordance with the Jewish practice of providing a watchman for the deceased prior to burial).

***

We are also seeing an explosion of Jews in genres where we least expect to find them. Animation, for example, is rife with Jews and Jewish themes – just look at the worlds created by Disney, Pixar and DreamWorks (owned by three Jews no less). DreamWorks' first movie after escaping Disney was *Prince of Egypt* (1998), an animated retelling of the Exodus from Egypt (complete with Val Kilmer as God) which also stuck closely to the sources. Was Jeffery Katzenberg of DreamWorks compelled by the historical parallel between his employment at Disney and that of the biblical Hebrews?

Beyond the Bible, there are Jewish bees, giraffes, lions, birds, and even food products. Consider *Shrek* (2001). Shrek was originally created by Jewish cartoonist William Steig and his name derives from the Yiddish word meaning fear or terror. *Shrek 2* (2004) was written by David N. Weiss, who, in interviews, explained that the film's basic theme (defining love as 'what's important to you is important to me') is based on some traditional Jewish wisdom that he had once heard from a rabbi.

If one wants to find the contemporary heir to Kafka's use of beetles, jackals, apes and mice to analogise the Jewish condition, then look no further than the animated movies featuring anthropomorphic animals and monsters: *Madagascar* (2005), *Rio* (2011), *Monsters, Inc.* (2001), *Monsters University* (2013), *Finding Nemo* (2003) and so on. These animals tend to dream of living beyond their immediate, typically urban, surroundings. But when their dreams come true, these animals cannot handle life in the wild. Their sensitive, intellectual natures make them unfit for what nature throws at them. These animals are city-slicking, wise-cracking and defined by their brains – or *yiddische kopf* (Jewish brains). In an echo of Gregor Samsa, animated Jewish animals yearn to be more human.

This idea even extends to toys. In the *Toy Story* films, none of the characters voiced by Jews are humanoid. They are not the cowboys, astronauts or soldiers (perhaps buying into long-held stereotypes about Jewish male physical inadequacy and their place in the world). Instead, they are a pair of potatoes, a dinosaur and a mythical one-horned horse. Mr and Mrs Potato Head are voiced by comedian Don Rickles and Estelle Harris (George Costanza's mum in *Seinfeld*) respectively. Mr Potato Head is the brainchild of Brooklyn-born toy inventor George Lerner, a Jew of Romanian descent. The Hassenfeld Brothers (later renamed Hasbro) sold the first Mr Potato Head as a kit of facial parts with the suggestion that a real potato was used. Elsewhere in the film, Wallace Shawn voices the sensitive and neurotic tyrannosaurus rex, Rex, whose character traits are stereotypically Jewish (and T. Rex was the name of Jewish rock star Marc Bolan's band). Stand-up comedian Jeff Garlin, who is famous for his role as Larry

David's agent/friend Jeff in *Curb Your Enthusiasm*, plays Buttercup, the white male unicorn, in *Toy Story 3* (2010).

In the 2016 cartoon *Sausage Party*, the metaphor is even extended to food-stuffs. Seth Rogen plays Frank, a sausage, yearning for the day when he will be bought by 'a god' (a customer) and be delivered to the promised land of 'The Great Beyond'. There, his wishes will come true, and he can (literally) enter his bun girlfriend, Brenda (Kirsten Wiig). Frank partners up with Palestinian flatbread Lavash (David Krumholtz) and Jewish bagel Sammy (Edward Norton), doing a curious impression of Woody Allen, including accent, incessant hand-wringing and worrying. Lavash and Sammy spend most of the movie bickering, with Lavash complaining that Sammy and his kosher ilk have taken over most of the 'West Shelf'. But, together with Frank, they learn that they are not the enemy, but that the humans are. The stratification of the real world is preserved and reflected in the supermarket one, and the film is full of stereotypes. By the end, *Sausage Party* proposes an unorthodox solution to the bagel-pitta conflict, and even a form of reconciliation between the mustard and the juice, as well as all the other conflicting foodstuffs.

But it is in the explosion of superhero movies, exploiting the back catalogues of DC and Marvel Comics, that has brought a slew of subsurface Jewish characters to the screen. These are characters who are nowhere identifiably Jewish but are based on Jewish tropes at their very creation. Their origins often have deep roots in Jewish lore, drawing on contemporary reincarnations of the famous legend of the Golem, a humanoid sculpted from clay and animated to do the bidding of the Maharal of Prague, Rabbi Judah Loew (1525–1609). They are the extension of the pattern in which Jewish comic book writers and artists created all-American superheroes who masked Jewish interiors. Superman is the greatest example, but the genre also includes Spiderman, the Hulk, Wonder Woman, the X-Men and their ilk.

Superheroes all have a coded Jewish history, whether they were invented by Jews or not. No amount of makeover can erase their core underlying Jewishness. To paraphrase the great American comedian Lenny Bruce: if you're a superhero, you're Jewish even if you're goyish. Typically, these characters tend to remain Jewish beneath the surface. Superman, as is well known, was the creation of two American Jews – Jerry Siegel and Joe Shuster – who conceived of him as a conceptually Jewish character. 'Clark Kent' is just a cover name, hiding an inner Jewishness. As Jewish novelist Michael Chabon wrote: 'Only a Jew would pick a name like that for himself.' Captain America was created by Jack Kirby (born Jacob Kurtzberg) and Joe Simon (born Hymie Simon), who wanted to create a new superhero to uphold American values in the face of the Nazi threat. He, too, hid beneath the non-Jewish name, 'Steve Rogers'. Wonder Woman – born

Diana, Princess of Themyscira, Daughter of Hippolyta – also hides under her assumed identity, 'Diana Prince'.

Usually, such characters are played by non-Jewish characters, making their subsurface Jewishness invisible to a mainstream audience unfamiliar with the history of superheroes. However, the *Spiderman* films directed by Jewish-American director Sam Raimi coupled with Andrew Garfield playing the title role in *The Amazing Spider-Man* (2012), returned the genre to its Jewish roots. Likewise, the casting of a Jewish actor in the titular role of *Wonder Woman* (2017) marks a departure from this past. Wonder Woman was played by model Gal Gadot, a former Miss Israel and IDF combat trainer who, uniquely, keeps her modern Israeli accent. Wonder Woman betrays other Jewish characteristics. In this movie, her quiet and bookish alter ego, Diana Prince, is an expert in ancient weapons, working at the Louvre museum in Paris – clearly an example of her *yiddische kopf*. She even wears a pair of glasses – a stereotypical movie marker of Jewishness. Wonder Woman is highly ethical. She looks to heal a fractured world, otherwise known in Judaism as *tikkun olam*, and adheres to a code of decency, known in Yiddish as *menschlikayt*. Wonder Woman is a fine, upright, honourable human being. She is an example of social justice. So, with the casting of Gal Gadot, now we have come full circle. From gentile origins, Wonder Woman is finally outed as Jewish. Played by an Israeli woman, her inner Jewishness is made explicit. Wonder Woman is surely an example of an '*eshet chayil*', a 'woman of valour' or, in other words, a tough Jewess with attitude.

Then there is the much darker 2019 film *Joker*, directed by Jewish filmmaker Todd Phillips, and starring Joaquin Phoenix. Born Arthur Fleck, Joker has a Jewish last name, and grows up in a Gotham apartment (recognisable as a New York slum).

Doctor Manhattan in *Watchmen* (2009) is a German-Jewish refugee who flees Nazi Germany. Born Jon Osterman, a watchmaker's son, he is transformed into an all-powerful and godlike being with superhuman powers. His name refers not to the city but to the Second World War project that developed the first atomic bombs, and which was a very Jewish endeavour.

Blending the genres of animation and superheroes are the *Transformers* movies (directed by the Jewish Michael Bay). Their facility at imitation and ability to change themselves taps into Kafka's *Metamorphosis* as well as that of the golem. The Transformers are giant robots who can transform into everyday objects, including cars, aeroplanes, trucks and tanks. The Transformers excel at mimicry. They switch between machine and robot with chameleonic-like ease, perfectly mimicking human-made cars, trucks, and the like. They have evolved their machine disguises as a tactic to move unnoticed among humans and travel around at will: embodying the struggle of Jews to blend into, and pass, in Western Christian society, to be invisible. The Transformers resemble Woody Allen's curious creation, Zelig, that commonplace chameleonic Jewish character, who is discovered for his remarkable ability to transform himself to resemble anyone he is near. Such imitation has long been felt to be mark the Jewish condition. For Max Horkheimer and Theodor Adorno, 'undisciplined mimicry' was 'engraved in the living substance of the dominated and passed down by a process of unconscious imitation in infancy from generation to generation, from the down-at-heel Jew to the rich banker'.

Superheroes and Transformers are symbolic Jews in space but more recently we have seen a growth in 'yiddische' astronauts. Of course, the original Star Wars trilogy featured a Jewish actor playing Han Solo (Harrison Ford) and Yoda (voiced by Frank Oz), whose name is Hebrew for 'knowledge'. Yoda is a blend of the biblical Methuselah, but talks like a Yiddish *alter kaka* (old person). We can also claim Carrie Fisher by lineage, so that makes Leia Organa – wait for it – a Jewish Alderaanian princess. And they all reappear in the more recent trilogy, rebooted by J.J. Abrams. Natalie Portman starred as Queen Amidala and Padme in George Lucas' *The Phantom Menace* (1999), although there were complaints that the representation of Watto, the slaveowner, was based on anti-Jewish stereotypes. One might consider that Abrams' involvement in the more recent trilogy has resurrected its subsurface Jewishness. Han Solo and Leia reappear, and, on the other side of the force, it is hard not to believe that Adam Driver, as Ben Solo (nom de guerre, Kylo Ren), in *The Force Awakens* (2015), *The Last Jedi* (2017) and *The Rise of Skywalker* (2019) is not Jewish. He is the son of Leia and Han.

Abrams also updated *Star Trek*, highlighting the submerged Jewishness of the original TV series for his sequel of *Star Trek* movies. It is commonly known that the cerebral, pacifist, intellectual Vulcans were conceived along Jewish lines and the Spock greeting sign is based on the raising of the hands during the priestly blessing. This was never made explicit in the films and Spock, the only non-human member of the USS *Enterprise* crew, thus functions as a symbolic or conceptual Jew.

Predators (2010) features Isabelle (Alice Braga) as a beautiful, gritty, and badass IDF sniper who is captured in an operation after her spotter is killed. She is transported to an alien planet where she and her male companions are hunted like prey by an alien species. Isabelle may well be the first serious Jewess in cinematic outer space!

When it comes to depicting antisemitism outside of the Holocaust, the line between Jewish victim and non-Jewish perpetrator is also being blurred. In 2001's *The Believer*, Ryan Gosling portrayed a self-hating *yeshiva bochur* (Jewish religious school student) whose internalised self-hatred leads him to becoming a highly articulate and intelligent neo-Nazi skinhead – who beats up the type of *yeshiva bochur* that he once was. In the same year, Arthur Miller's little-known novel about American antisemitism, *Focus* (which he wrote in 1945), was adapted into a film. Lawrence Newman (William H. Macy) is an antisemite forced by his boss to buy a new pair of glasses and is mistaken for a Jew. Subsequently, he becomes the victim of prejudice – which was alive and well in the United States at the time the movie was set in 1945, culminating in violence whereby he has to defend himself alongside the Jewish shopkeeper Finkelstein (David Paymer).

Denial (2016) is based on the true-life courtroom travails of the American Jewish historian Deborah Lipstadt (played by Rachel Weisz), who was sued for libel by notorious Holocaust denier David Irving. But this well-meaning film manages to emphasise the charm of Irving, as played by Timothy Spall, versus the relative lack of it in the character of Lipstadt who comes across as drab and dull, evoking more sympathy for the non-Jew, who is presented as the victim! Most troublingly, one short establishing shot depicting a Jewish driveway in north London filled with expensive cars managed to produce a lazy and offensive stereotype of rich Jews that detracts from the film's anti-antisemitism stance.

In a completely different vein, Sasha Baron Cohen's *Borat* (2006) and *Borat Subsequent Moviefilm: Delivery of Prodigious Bribe to American Regime for Make Benefit Once Glorious Nation of Kazakhstan* (2020) both exposed and mocked contemporary antisemitism. As the titular Borat Sagdiyev, Sacha Baron Cohen played a Jew-hating, yet paradoxically Hebrew-speaking, Kazakh reporter. (Did Baron Cohen speak Hebrew because he correctly calculated that most audiences would not know it wasn't Kazakh, or was it a nod and wink to his Jewish audiences to say, 'It's okay, I'm kosher'?). His Borat displayed a consistent irreverence towards topics and subject matter where other Jews have traditionally feared to tread. Never one to walk on a tightrope of political correctness, he always crosses the line. Every ancient, anti-Jewish stereotype is lampooned.

His unique journalistic style exposed and mocked contemporary antisemitism, easing open utterances of prejudice. In one scene, he had customers at a country and western bar enthusiastically sing along to his ditty, 'Throw the Jew down the well'. The film was saturated with other representations of antisemitism. The 'Running of the Jew' sequence has got to be one of the most imaginative Jewish moments ever conceived. Here, in a carnivalesque public event, mimicking the running of the bulls in Pamplona, Spain, the crowd waves money at giant and gross caricatures of a Jewish couple. The female 'Mrs Jew' lays a 'Jew egg' which is then crushed by the participating children before the 'Jew chick hatches'. It predicted the real-life floats at a Belgian carnival in 2019 and 2020, which drew ire because of their blatantly antisemitic caricatures of ultra-Orthodox Jews – in the 2019 float they are surrounded by piles of money. Borat concludes his 'report' with the words that his country has a problem, 'economic, social and Jew'.

In the sequel, Borat explains how the 'Running of the Jew' has been cancelled. 'All we have left is Holocaust Remembrance Day,' he mourns over footage of a party full of young people dancing while covered in soap suds, 'where we commemorate our heroic soldiers who ran the camps'.

Borat again deploys his unique journalistic style to expose and mock contemporary antisemitism, easing open utterances of prejudice or, at least, a willingness to turn a blind eye towards it. At a hardware store, he asks the owner if propane gas will finish a gypsy in a van. 'How many gypsies could I finish with one canister?' he inquires. When he asks for a canister to finish the lives of twenty gypsies, the man recommends the next size up. Borat also buys a large cake and asks the lady behind the counter to pipe the white supremacist slogan, 'Jews will not replace us', in icing on it, along with a smiley face. She willingly obliges. Because Borat wants his daughter, Tutar, to have a complete makeover to make her more attractive to Mike Pence, he consults a plastic surgeon who recommends a rhinoplasty. 'What's wrong with my nose? Do I look like a Jew?' Tutar asks. The surgeon assures her she does not. Borat is relieved. But then the surgeon explains how Jews look, making a grotesque gesture around his nose. Borat extends the gesture, exaggerating the alleged Jewish nose even further and the surgeon concurs that 'it can be that bad' for a Jewish person.

On her voyage of self-discovery, from repressed Kazakh to liberated woman, Tutar eventually discovers Holocaust denial on social media. Via Facebook she learns that 'our nation's proudest moment, the Holocaust, never happened'. 'How dare you say that,' Borat replies angrily. Feeling 'very depressed', Borat wants to commit suicide. But he cannot afford to buy a gun. So, in one of those lines that is delivered so quickly and straight that it is another blink-and-you'll-miss-it moment, he decides to go 'to the nearest synagogue to wait for the next mass shooting'.

Turning up at Temple Kol Emeth, he is 'disguised as a typical Jew'. This involves a long fake Pinocchio-type nose, a fake bag of money, with Satanic wings on his back, and a puppet on a string. As he enters, he greets an elderly Jewish Holocaust survivor with the words, 'Very nice weather we have been controlling.' She hugs and kisses him, and Borat worries out loud that her Jewish venom might be a slow-releasing toxin. When he tells her that 'the Holocaust didn't happen' and is a 'fairy tale', she reassures him that 'I saw it with my own eyes', much to his clear delight. 'The Holocaust happened, really? Thank you, Judith. You make me so happy!'

The standout film on this topic was, ironically, made by a non-Jew. Spike Lee's *BlacKkKlansman* (2018) is based on the true story of the black cop Ron Stallworth who infiltrated the Ku Klux Klan by using his Jewish partner to act as his front. Philip 'Flip' Zimmerman, played by Adam Driver, is the Jewish cop who thinks nothing of his background until his partner reminds him that he 'has skin in the game'. Eventually, the two team up in a Black-Jewish alliance and the movie ends movingly but fittingly with the Charlottesville, Virginia rally when neo-Nazis openly chanted 'Jew will not replace us'. More than one person was brought to tears in the cinema where I watched it.

Biblical themes infuse many of these and other films. The title character of *Mad Max: Fury Road*, as played by Tom Hardy, is another Moses-like saviour. By replacing the original Max, who was played by Mel Gibson, the film is apologising for his unrepentantly antisemitic vision in *The Passion of the Christ* (2004) (itself a form of 'gorno', preparing the United States for the War on Terror). The *Transformers* films also reference the Exodus from Egypt. Like the Jews, they are wandering, nomadic migrants, settling on Earth where they are treated like outsiders and pariahs, forced to hide in plain sight. According to *Transformers* (2007) writer Roberto Orci, the film's central theme is 'being away from home and adapting to a new world'. There are themes of Armageddon, and particularly David vs. Goliath, as the humans take on the Decepticons. Michael Bay has described the tone of the films as the biblical epic '*Ben-Hur* fused with *Apocalypse Now*'.

Ben-Hur was itself remade in 2016 as part of a mini-revival of the biblical epic that includes Ridley Scott's terrible *Exodus: Of Gods and Kings* (2014) in which God was voiced by an eleven-year-old prepubescent British child with a speech impediment, as well as more interesting productions by director Darren Aronofsky.

In Aronofsky's *The Fountain* (2006), a cerebral science fiction film that aims to push the boundaries of the genre while dealing with the big philosophical questions about life, death and eternity, Aronofsky directed his then wife, Rachel Weisz. He described his film as 'the search for God, the search for meaning'. It opens with a direct quote from Genesis 3:24 and thereafter is designed around the Sefirot of Kabbalah. He deals with Jewishness explicitly in *Noah* (2014), which was an unambiguous version of the biblical story, drawing upon Genesis, Midrash and the Book of Enoch. His follow-up *mother!* (2017) divided audiences, even earning loud boos as well as applause. Marketed by Paramount Pictures as a horror film, it defies genre conventions and audience expectations. It is in a genre all its own: allegorical biblical movie, building upon the Midrashic mode showed in his *Noah*, in which a poet called Him (Javier Bardem) and his unnamed wife (Jennifer Lawrence) are renovating his childhood home. A series of uninvited guests arrive – graciously received by Him much to his wife's consternation – and leading to death, mayhem, carnage and an all-consuming fire in which all but Him die. The film ends as it begins: with an image of a woman awaking in bed, repeating the cycle.

But the standout Jewish film which works around the Bible and towers above the rest is the Coen brothers' 2009 *A Serious Man*. While Jewish characters crop up here and there in the brother's other works, such as Bob Dylan in *Inside Llewyn Davis* (2013) and in the hilarious interfaith discussion in *Hail, Caesar!* (2016), none are as extended and rounded as those found in the 2009 movie. The film which has had rabbis, theologians and academics debating it ever since. Is it about the biblical character Job? Is it about quantum mechanics? Is he, or is he not, a *dybbuk*? What is a *dybbuk*? What is the fable of the goy's teeth? And what does it all mean? Their refusal to answer has left us scratching our heads – they were just messing with us – but in so doing produced a wonderful tribute to the Jewish world they grew up in, as well as a prologue that could be a 3D Marc Chagall painting.

A Serious Man is the film that is closest, in spirit, to Stanley Kubrick's Talmudic film style. Although it is explicitly Jewish – something Kubrick never managed to achieve in his lifetime – it holds an abundance of unexplained religious references rooted in Jewish lore. The film opens with an epigraph from the medieval Jewish sage and commentator Rashi: 'Receive with simplicity everything that happens to you.' Are the Coens misleading us here? Or are they warning us merely to enjoy the experience and not think about it too deeply? It certainly shows their knowledge of Jewish philosophy (recall that Walter Sobchack's dog in their earlier *The Big Lebowski* was called 'Maimonides' and 'Jew by choice' Walter was fond of quoting the father of modern Zionism, Theodore Herzl).

The film then launches into a subtitled Yiddish-language prologue set in a Polish *shtetl* concerning the spirit of a *dybbuk*. This prologue may or may not have a connection with what happens next. The person in question may or may not be a *dybbuk*. We are never entirely clear. In a fashion mirroring the match cut in Kubrick's *2001: A Space Odyssey* (1968), which accelerates us four million years into the future, the Coens fast-forward us into the 1960s, where the next language heard is untranslated Hebrew. And while English dominates the dialogue thereafter, it is punctuated with further untranslated Hebrew and Yiddish phrases (*goy, Hashem, get*). On one level, *A Serious Man* is a variant of the Book of Job. Its *schlemiel* protagonist is Larry, as he undergoes his own personal ordeal, shuffling from rabbi to rabbi to make sense of what is happening to him, and we end the film none the wiser. A fable about a goy's teeth – much like the prologue – goes nowhere. Or maybe it does.

★★★

In the past two decades, the numbers and types of Jews on screen have proliferated. There are the repeats of some old stereotypes, but these are joined by new ones with a twist. For me, the most interesting developments are not those films that are obviously Jewish on the surface but those in which the Jewishness is submerged, inferred or where Jewishness is not the whole point of the story but an incidental, surplus addition. Increasingly, filmmakers do not even try to explain the Jewish references; they are unapologetically Jewish. They include Jewish references in a way they were not before, so there is less self-explaining about being Jewish (especially in American films).

In twenty years, the Jews we are seeing are no longer just Jew-ish, relegated to a mere shrug or sigh or Old-World accent, but are much more rounded characters. It is a sign that Jews are more comfortable in their own skin and can be detached and self-critical about their beliefs and, for example, attitudes towards Israel, particularly as some have become more disillusioned with the country. There is also a sense of detachment from the Holocaust. Younger Jewish filmmakers, in short, are more relaxed about their identity.

But the fallout from the Donald Trump years, as well as Brexit and other manifestations of populism around the world, have yet to be fully felt. Given the resulting rise in antisemitism, there will be greater nervousness and retrenchment, less of a desire to question and show the uglier side. Only time will tell.

Meanwhile, as Israeli television spreads around the globe, so the number of films from Israel will multiply, presenting an even more nuanced perspective, particularly from the point of view of religion and orthodoxy. There will also be a greater challenge to the presentation of the Ashkenazi way of life as the cinematic norm for Jewishness. Already, we are seeing greater representation of Sephardi, Mizrahi and other forms of Jewishness and Judaism, as well as their perspective, in films such as 2011's *El Gusto*, which tells the story of Jewish and Muslim Algerian musicians, or 2015's *Blue Like Me*, about Mumbai's Jewish community. It will be interesting to see if this influences Jewish cinema globally.

It is hard to predict with any accuracy what we shall see in the future, other than a medley of representation that will hopefully begin to do justice to the full colour and variety of Jewish life, especially nonnormative, nonbinary, female and non-Ashkenazic.

APPENDIX 1: BIBLIOGRAPHICAL NOTE

The inspiration for this essay has been my book, published in 2012, *The New Jew in Film: Exploring Jews and Jewishness in Contemporary Cinema* (IB Tauris). I have supplemented it with various blog posts and articles for such publications as *Ha'aretz* and *The Forward* over the years since then. It is also their regular coverage of new Jewish films by other writers that has helped me to update my original research. Alas, because there has been no sequel to my book nor any comprehensive book covering Jewish film from 2011 until the present, I recommend turning to the Jewish press, as well as such academic journals as *Jewish Film and New Media* (published by Wayne State University Press), for the latest research into Jewish film. I also recommend keeping up with the regular Jewish film festivals around the world for the latest information on Jewish film.

FROM THE *JR* ARCHIVE

'TALKING FILMS', BY GALI GOLD

In this essay from JR*'s October 2008 issue, Gali Gold explored how Israeli cinema of the new millennium was addressing previously unexplored issues – not always to the taste of its home audience.*

At the time of writing, Gali Gold was the Artistic Director of the UK Jewish Film Festival. She is now Head of Cinema at London's Barbican Centre.

The first shots of Nurit Aviv's latest documentary, *Sacred Language, Spoken Language* (2008) are taken from Alexandre Promio's footage filmed from the train from Jerusalem to Jaffa in 1897. These pioneering experiments, initiated by the Lumière Brothers, took place as cinema celebrated its birth as the seventh art. In the same year, another dramatic event took place. The first Zionist Congress was held in Basel, and the national movement of Zionism, with its dream of a secular return of the Jews to their biblical Promised Land, was born.

For many years after the establishment of Israel, it seemed as if the simultaneous birth of cinema and state was of no significance to the Zionist leadership. Israel's founding fathers were never much impressed by the moving image. While for other revolutionary leaders (notably in the Soviet sphere) cinema was a powerful tool for the indoctrination of the masses, David Ben-Gurion and his partners were far less enthusiastic, staying loyal to other literary forms.

Even though it was at pains to establish itself as a secular movement, Zionism relied heavily on the biblical and religious foundations of Judaism. Film scholars tend to attribute the reluctance of the movement's leaders to exploit film to the ancient prohibition against creation of graven image combined with the unique importance attached to the text itself. It may well be that these two factors lay behind the failure to invest (materially, artistically or critically) in film during the early decades of the Israeli state.

Films were nevertheless always made in Israel and, as in other countries, they serve as a fascinating window on society's conscious and less conscious lives, but it is in the new millennium that they are really achieving recognition.

As Israeli cinema gains unprecedented acclaim internationally and at home, it is precisely the Jewish aspect of Israeli lives – the 'return of the repressed' – that emerges as one of its novelties. In the last few years, we have had the popular hit *Ushpizin* (Gidi Dar, 2004); the tragic family drama *My Father, My Lord* (David Volach, 2007); the coming-of-age narrative *Tehilim* (Raphael Nadjari, 2007); the woman-centred piece *The Secrets* (Avi Nesher, 2007); and the recent poetic essay documentary *Sacred Language, Spoken Language*.

Filmmakers are tackling religious belief head-on: the frictions between religious and secular lives; the inherent tension between individual freedom and divine supervision and the complex impact of the holy language, as it was transformed to embrace the profane, when Hebrew became Israel's common language.

This trend by professional filmmakers is accompanied by a growing enthusiasm for cinema amongst national-religious youngsters (those observant Jews who embrace the Zionist project). They are increasingly opting for careers in film and TV, most notably through the acclaimed Ma'ale School for Film and TV in Jerusalem. In recent years, graduates have presented work at the prestigious international film festivals, daring to explore controversial themes such as sexuality (*Ve'Ahavta/And Thou Shalt Love,* Chaim Elbaum, 2008); women's status in Jewish religion and common law and its impact on women's social and family status (notable examples are the celebrated documentaries by Anat Zuria, *Purity,* 2002 and *Sentenced to Marriage,* 2004); as well as issues such as divorce, single parenting and even circumcision.

Jewish religion, faith and affiliation and their relation to Israeli identity are being explored and expressed through cinema rather than being used as tools to restrict this expression. In this way, the void created in the first five decades of Israeli cinema by the failure to engage with such topics is now populated by dramas and documentaries that bring these issues to the fore.

Another notable development in Israeli cinema is the recent more frequent willingness to present dialogue in other languages, despite Hebrew having dominated Israeli films for decades. In Dover Kosashvili's popular *Late Marriage* (2001), one hears Georgian no less than Hebrew as the charming love story exploring a close-knit Georgian community in an Israeli suburb unfolds.

Moroccan, French and Hebrew are heard throughout the recent acclaimed chamber piece *Shivah/Seven Days* (Ronit and Shlomi Elkabetz, 2008) as we spend the traditional seven days of mourning amongst a Jewish family of Moroccan descent when one of seven siblings has suddenly passed away.

Language as a cultural barrier and potential bridge takes a central role in *The Band's Visit* (Eran Kolirin, 2007), in which an Egyptian police orchestra is stranded in an isolated Israeli town, somewhere in the southern desert.

The local residents, all clearly of Middle Eastern origin but no longer fluent in Arabic, their ancestors' mother tongue, must turn to the West and use English as the only possible common language between them and the unexpected visitors. The intimacy that develops between the Israelis and Egyptians during a single weekend, and the emergence of shared values and interests brings home to the audience the similarities between the two groups. It is a powerful testament to the link between the neighbouring societies and the frequently overlooked status of Israel as an integral part of the Middle East. The play of languages and the innovative use of English highlights both what has been lost by these neighbouring cultures, and the potential gains.

Adding another layer to the politics of sound, the cast of the film are all Israelis, Jews and Arabs, who share the Middle East as their cultural heritage. The decision of the Academy of Motion Picture to disqualify *The Band's Visit* from being Israel's nominee for the Oscars this year, on the grounds that there was too little use of the state's official languages, is ironic, overlooking as it does the film's authentic expression of one of the most significant features of the Israeli 'state'.

Fascinating additions to the trend of openness to linguistic diversity are *Ashkenaz* (Rachel Leah-Jones, 2007), a documentary which, while looking at the complexities of Israel's ethnic economies, gives voice to the recent yearning for Yiddish as a lost language, sacrificed on the altar of Modern Hebrew, and *Homeland* (Dani Rosenberg, 2008), a brand new Israeli feature drama in Yiddish.

Through this audio landscape, another significant minority of Israeli society gains visibility and a new form of recognition. A growing number of dramas and documentaries are by Palestinian-Israelis. Here Arabic, with a unique amalgam of Hebrew vocabulary and slang, embodies the often hybrid identities of the filmmakers and of the film subjects. Prominent filmmakers include Hany Abu Assad with *Nazareth 2000* (2000), *Ford Transit* (2002) and *Paradise Now* (2005); Tawfik Abu Wael with *Atash/Thirst* (2004); Ibtisam Mara'ana with *Paradise Lost* (2003); *Three Times Divorced* (2007) and Rokaya Sabbah with *On Hold* (2007).

Another interesting aspect of recent Israeli cinema is the way films engage with the Israeli place. Here, there is a divide between those films (mainly documentaries) that position themselves broadly within the periphery of Israeli society and on its multiple negotiated borders and those dramas (mainly urban) that shy away from important aspects of Israel's geopolitics.

In the first category come *Paradise Lost*; *Wall*; *The Syrian Bride*; *9 Star Hotel* and *Lemon Tree*. Rooted in the territory of the Middle East, these films probe and reflect the heterogeneity of the land and its people.

In the second category are *Broken Wings*; *Joy*; *Jellyfish*; *The Bubble*; *Foul Gesture* and *Noodle*. Although these cinematic stories are not free from trouble and complexities, they have a much narrower focus, which does not extend beyond the Israeli Jewish collective.

As far as local audiences are concerned, there is hardly a doubt as to which of these scenarios has more appeal. Israeli Jews celebrate their cinema with far greater enthusiasm when it offers charming journeys into the local culture while staying bound to a dominant Jewish point of view.

A case in point is Eran Riklis's recent feature *Lemon Tree* (2008), based on true events, which tells the story of a Palestinian widow whose lemon grove is about to be uprooted by the Israeli army due to its proximity to the newly built home of Israel's Minister of Defence. The film not only demonstrates the tragedy and ironies of the territorial conflict between the Israelis and the Palestinians but also presents a unique and rare Palestinian point of view on the course of events. While the film follows the courageous battle of a farmer to save her livelihood, it gently establishes a powerful relationship between her and the minister's wife, one that transcends language, culture and other, more literal, barriers.

Lemon Tree captured the hearts of audiences across Europe, picked up the Audience Award at the Berlin Film Festival and is currently playing to the international festival circuit. However, it failed to reach out to Israelis on its home turf.

It would be wrong to conclude that Israeli cinema audiences are looking only for escapism. *Waltz with Bashir* (2008), Ari Folman's animated documentary dealing with the filmmaker's attempt to restore his memories of the 1982 Lebanon war, was highly successful in Israel as well as being the talk of the day at Cannes. However, the films that win the hearts of the majority of Israeli cinemagoers are those that gaze inward and backward into the many origins of Israeli identity: its Jewish origins, its different diasporas, its national wars.

Films which breach the boundaries of these essentially Jewish narratives, or provide competing narratives, are a part of the recent local cinematic proliferation, but the major part of their audience is still found outside Israel.

'NEW WAVE', BY DAVID HERMAN

In JR*'s April 2019 issue, David Herman assessed the impact of the powerful new Israeli dramas sweeping across the world's TV screens. Positing this trend alongside a similar wave of Israeli fiction and new technology, he asked if this burst of creativity heralds a fresh way of exploring Israeli identity.*

David Herman is a regular JR *contributor and writes for the* Guardian *and the* New Statesman, *among other publications. He has also produced TV programmes on the Holocaust and related subjects for BBC and Channel 4.*

The recent death of Amos Oz marked a turning point in Israeli culture. He was part of the same generation as Aharon Appelfeld, A.B. Yehoshua and Joshua Sobol, all born in the 1930s. For as long as I can remember, discussions of Israeli culture were dominated by talk of serious novels about the State of Israel. Suddenly, all this is changing. A new Israeli culture is exploding on the scene, producing best-selling nonfiction, hit television shows on Netflix and a different kind of writing.

The biggest impact has been on television – not just within Israel but internationally. Israeli culture is finding new audiences abroad, especially in the most important market of all, America.

This started less than ten years ago with the drama series *Prisoners of War* (*Hatufim*), which originally aired in Israel in 2010. It told the story of three Israeli soldiers who were captured 17 years before while on a secret mission with their unit in Lebanon. When it was shown in Israel, *Hatufim* had the highest ratings of any Israeli TV drama.

You have probably never heard of *Prisoners of War* but you may well have heard of the American spin-off, *Homeland*, a huge TV hit in the US and in Britain, starring Damian Lewis, Claire Danes and Mandy Patinkin and now into its eighth season. *Homeland* has won huge critical acclaim and numerous awards.

On the basis of *Homeland*, Gideon Raff, the creator of *Prisoners of War*, produced a number of series for US television, including *Tyrant* (which ran on FX for three seasons) about an ordinary American family caught up in the mayhem of the Middle East; *Dig* (on USA Network), an archaeological thriller about an FBI agent stationed in Jerusalem; and last year's hit, *The Spy*, with Sacha Baron Cohen as Eli Cohen, who was a real-life Israeli spy in the Middle East in the 1950s and 1960s (on Canal Plus/Netflix).

On Israeli TV, the success of *Prisoners of War* was quickly followed by the drama *Fauda*. This series revolved around a team of undercover Israeli soldiers battling Palestinian terrorists. Two seasons were aired in Israel before it was taken up by Netflix. The *New York Times* voted *Fauda* the best international TV show of 2017. Like *Prisoners of War*, *Fauda* owed much of its success to the camaraderie of a close-knit team of Israeli soldiers but also showed that the real casualties, on both sides, were the women. The series was clearly pro-Israel but the Palestinian characters were not one-dimensional villains and were given time to develop.

Another Israeli drama, *When Heroes Fly* (2018), is now showing in the UK on Netflix. It tells the story of a group of veterans of the 2006 Lebanon War who, a decade later, reunite for a final mission – to rescue the girlfriend of one of the soldiers who has been kidnapped by a drug cartel in Colombia. The show is based on a novel by the Israeli author Amir Gutfreund and features Tomer Kapon, one of the stars from *Fauda*. It starts as a conventional war film, but then moves to South America and becomes a story of drug cartels and a strange cult. But in the last episodes it really takes off and becomes a moving reflection on time, memory and comradeship.

What is striking about these series, and perhaps what explains their appeal to British and American audiences, is how dark they are. There is no glorification of war. People suffer from PTSD. War haunts soldiers for years. Characters include Israeli drug dealers and gangsters, corrupt Israeli officials and cops out for revenge. The central characters are Israelis fighting Hezbollah and Palestinian terrorists, but they could just as well be veterans from the wars in Iraq and Afghanistan. We have had Scandi-noir, about detectives hunting serial killers. This is Israeli-noir, about IDF veterans haunted by memories of war.

The success of these dramas has opened the way for other genres. *The Beauty and the Baker* (which aired two seasons in 2013 and 2017) is a love story about an ordinary baker in Tel Aviv who still lives at home with his parents and falls in love with one of the richest and most beautiful women in Israel. A sort of Israeli version of *Notting Hill*, it has aired in more than 200 countries and is now available on Amazon Prime.

Two other recent shows are also making waves. *Shtisel*, a series that focuses on ultra-Orthodox Jews in Jerusalem, is currently airing on Netflix in the UK. The series interweaves the human stories of a large family: Giti is abandoned by her husband and left to cope with five children; her brother, Akiva, seeks love with the help of a delightful matchmaker. It has been such a hit in the US that there is talk of an Amazon spin-off set in Brooklyn.

Another Netflix documentary being shown in the US is *One of Us*, which follows three former Hasidic Jews from Brooklyn who struggle with being ostracised from their former community.

What is interesting about these series is that they introduce the little-known world of ultra-Orthodox Jews to mainstream TV. Netflix in the States has also aired *The Wedding Plan*, Rama Burshtein's 2016 film about a quirky Orthodox woman in her 30s seeking a husband within the Orthodox community. At a time of growing antisemitism on both sides of the Atlantic, such programmes do a great deal to humanise Orthodox Jews. They also humanise Israelis, not by demonising Arabs or Palestinians, but by highlighting issues of love, family and ordinary communal life.

What is striking is that these dramas don't appear on the BBC or ITV. They appear on Netflix and Amazon Prime, inspire American spin-offs and are starting to feature international stars such as Sacha Baron Cohen. This is having an effect on Israeli cinema too, which has been marginalised for years in film festivals and art cinemas: in January it was announced that Karen Gillan (familiar to *Doctor Who* fans as Amy Pond) would star in *Gunpowder Milkshake*, a new assassin movie scripted by Israeli writer Ehud Lavski and due for release in 2020.

The portrayal of Israeli life offered in these dramas is often young, fast-paced and increasingly high-tech.

I don't suppose many people picked up on the following news story, which appeared in *Jane's Defence Weekly* last August. It stated: 'The United Kingdom has procured the Israeli-developed Drone Dome counter-unmanned aircraft system (C-UAS), manufacturer Rafael confirmed to *Jane's* on 13 August.' Four months later the story's resonance became clear when it was revealed that the military equipment used to stop further drone disruption at Gatwick Airport included the Israel-developed Drone Dome system, which can detect and jam communications between a drone and its operators.

And Israeli tech is expanding into other areas: many drivers in the UK and US use Waze GPS navigation, which was developed by the Israeli company Waze Mobile. In 2013 Google bought Waze for $966 million to add social data to its mapping business. Waze's 100 employees received over $1 million on average, the largest payout to employees in Israeli high tech.

This new high-tech Israel looms large in Dov Alfon's gripping thriller, *A Long Night in Paris* (2016), which has just been published in the UK. It's a compelling read about the kidnapping of an Israeli software manager at Charles de Gaulle Airport. Soon the bodies start to pile up as Israeli intelligence, Chinese hitmen and the French police get involved. What is distinctive about Alfon's novel, which moves between Paris and Israel, is the hyper-modern, high-tech feel. Abadi, from Israeli intelligence, is given a new gizmo: 'a new kind of smartphone with tracking capabilities, the brainchild of 8200's technology centre. Code-named "Navran", the communications device was the fastest he had experienced and it came with its own encryption system.'

Alfon's thriller is part of the exciting new wave of Israeli fiction. The recent deaths of Appelfeld and Oz are a reminder of the passing of writers who were formed by the Holocaust and the vicissitudes of the State of Israel. A new generation is finding its voice. These writers were born in the 1960s and 1970s: Alfon, Amir Gutfreund (who died tragically young at 52), Etgar Keret, Eshkol Nevo, Nir Baram and Ayelet Gundar-Goshen, who is still in her 30s and has just had her third novel, *Liar*, published in English. It's a generation formed by Israel's wars of 1967 and 1973 and the aftermath.

Like their predecessors, they often write about Israel, but from a different angle. Gutfreund's 2005 novel, *The World a Moment Later*, tells the story of pre-war Palestine and the new state of Israel from the 1920s to the 1970s, but it offers what Gutfreund calls 'A Shadow History of Israel'. A novel of huge ambition, it takes the conventional milestones of Palestinian and Israeli history but observes them through the stories of people who built the country but never became famous.

Eshkol Nevo's first novel, *Homesick* (2008), was on the Israeli bestseller list for 60 weeks and won two major prizes. His second novel, *World Cup Wishes*, is better still. The novel starts out as a kind of Israeli version of the TV sitcom *Friends*. Four young, quirky men fall in love, out of love, marry, have children, put up with each other's eccentricities. Some characters are preoccupied with what's happening to the Palestinians, and there's a sharp sense of the growing brutalisation of Israeli society. One character, Yuval, is tormented by memories of an incident he witnessed during his military service. Increasingly, the question becomes more pressing: Is there a future for such decent men in Israel?

Nir Baram's novel, *Good People*, received critical acclaim and sold 35,000 copies when it was published in Israel in 2010. It is an outstanding novel, moving between Nazi Germany and Stalin's Soviet Union, between Kristallnacht and the German invasion of the Soviet Union in 1941. Its strength lies in its originality.

There are no clichés in Baram's account of Nazism. His Nazis and Stalinists are interesting, ambitious young men playing office politics, trying to rise up the greasy pole to promotion.

This younger generation is preoccupied with history. Israeli history is always there; as Gutfreund has said, 'What a burden it is to be born both Jewish and Israeli – it's like carrying five watermelons on your back all your life.' But they interweave this preoccupation with the lives of their young characters, so the feeling is very different from the novels of Oz or Grossman.

But the recent publishing sensation from Israel is Yuval Noah Harari. He is not a novelist but a young academic who teaches at the Hebrew University in Jerusalem. His ambitious trilogy – *Sapiens: A Brief History of Humankind* (2014), *Homo Deus: A Brief History of Tomorrow* (2016), and *21 Lessons for the 21st Century* (2018) – have brought him international fame.

Also based in Jerusalem is the essayist Benjamin Balint, who has written an interesting book on *Commentary* magazine, a superb essay on Gershom Scholem, and a book, *Kafka's Last Trial* (published in the UK in January). Balint's book is an acclaimed account of the legal battle over Kafka's papers and asks: do the papers belong in Germany because Kafka was the greatest modern writer in German or should they be kept in Israel, because that's where Max Brod fled when the Germans marched into Prague?

Another Israeli academic, Malachi Hacohen, is professor of history, political science and religion at Duke University in North Carolina but was born and brought up in Israel. Hacohen is the author of the superb biography *Karl Popper – The Formative Years, 1902–1945* (2002). His forthcoming work, *Jacob & Esau: Jewish European History Between Nation and Empire*, is an ambitious attempt to offer an alternative Jewish European history that incorporates Jews into the development of Europe but doesn't tell their story as an exclusively Jewish one.

These books are not narrow academic monographs. They are works of intellectual and cultural history that have had a big impact in the UK and in America. They are very Jewish but tell a larger story about major 20th-century ideas.

There is a common link between this wave of TV dramas, fiction and histories of ideas: they are by Israelis, and are often set in Israel, but they strive – and succeed – in reaching a larger international audience. They are not just presenting an alternative face of Israel in order to promote 'soft power' and a more human face of the state than we are used to seeing in British and American media. They offer unsettling stories with a moral complexity that is very different from the stereotype of the typical 'sabra', and these dark tales resonate with international audiences, who are themselves going through dark times.

Israelis are finding a distinctive new voice that is dramatic, high-tech and intellectual. Whether it is on Netflix and Amazon Prime, navigating your car or in your local bookshop, it's here, now, enriching your life.

BlacKkKlansman, 2018, directed by Spike Lee, with John David Washington and Laura Harrier. (Photo 12 / Alamy Stock Photo)

A Serious Man, 2009, directed by Joel and Ethan Coen, with Michael Stuhlbarg and Sari Lennick. (ScreenProd / Photononstop / Alamy Stock Photo)

The Fountain, 2006, directed by Darren Aronofsky, with Hugh Jackman. (TCD / Prod.DB / Alamy Stock Photo)

Noah, 2014, directed by Darren Aronofsky, with, from left to right: Leo McHugh Carrol, Jennifer Connelly, Douglas Booth and Emma Watson. (AF archive / Alamy Stock Photo)

Vanessa Paloma Elbaz in her performance work *Seas of Change*, May 2001. The image on the screen shows the Edict of Expulsion with a photograph of three generations of Paloma Elbaz's grandmothers. (Ann Sherman)

A Jew and a Muslim playing chess from the *Book of Games, Chess, Dice and Boards*, folio 63r, 1282, commissioned by Alphonse X of Castile, 1283, in the Real Biblioteca del Monasterio de El Escorial, Madrid, Spain. (Album / Alamy Stock Photo)

Israeli singer–songwriter Idan Raichel at the MITO SettembreMusica Festival in Milan, Italy, 2015. (Rodolfo Sassano / Alamy Stock Photo)

Neta Elkayam performing at the Temple Synagogue, Krakow, Poland during the 27th Jewish Culture Festival in Krakow, 2017. (Courtesy Jewish Culture Festival, Krakow. Photo: Michal Ramus)

Israeli–Yemenite band A-WA, at the festival du Bout du Monde, Crozon, France, 2016. (Loic Venance / AFP via Getty Images)

Yair Dalal. (Courtesy of Yair Dalal)

From the graphic novel *The Wolf of Baghdad* by Carol Isaacs, 2020, published by Myriad Editions. (Carol Isaacs)

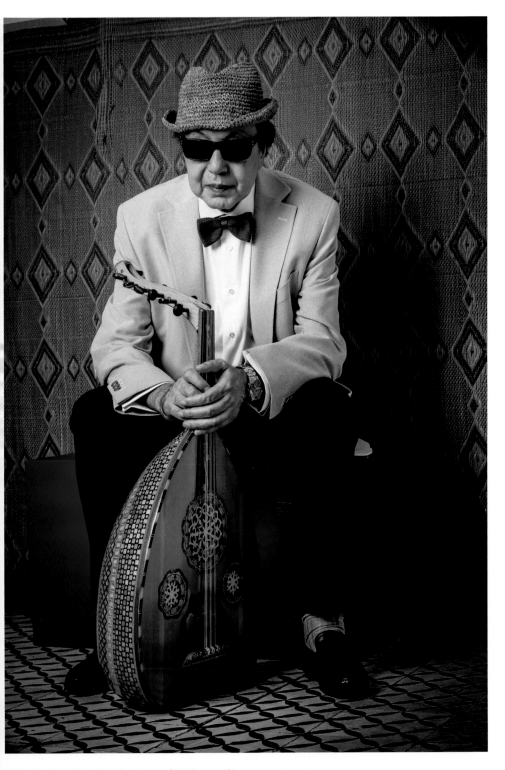

Haim Botbol. (Erradi / Courtesy of FTG records)

Cover of *Jewish Renaissance*, April 2011, featuring Iranian-American singer Galeet Dardashti. Cover design: Becky Redman; cover image: Galeet Dardashti; photo: Brian Tamborello)

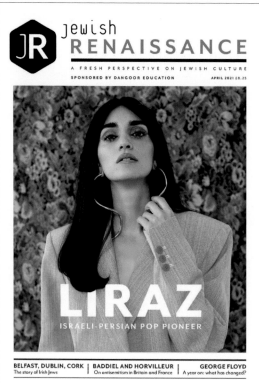

Cover of *Jewish Renaissance*, April 2021, featuring Israeli-Persian singer Liraz. (Cover design: Becky Redman; photo: Shai Franco)

THE BRIGHT SIDE OF IDENTITY: MUSIC, CROSSING BORDERS AND THE WAR ON TERROR

VANESSA PALOMA ELBAZ

On the morning of 11 September 2001, I got an early morning phone call from a voice student who was due to come for a private lesson at 10 a.m. He was in a state of shock about what was unfolding on his TV screen. I was living in Los Angeles and the three-hour time difference meant that the news of New York's twin towers falling, the attack on the Pentagon and the crashed aeroplane in a field in Pennsylvania had made it to Los Angelenos with our morning coffee. It was unfathomable to see people flinging themselves out of the buildings, or the crumbling of the second tower into a plume of black smoke. I recognised the feeling of emotional horror, numbness to the immensity of it and paralysing fear from my adolescence in Colombia. I knew that morning that America would start to understand the difficulties that people living with terrorism had known for years and that the mechanisms to confront its existential questions would soon emerge.

I was confronted with the searing pain that violence garners – but the call from my music student also reminded me of something else – of the importance of art and music in pinpointing what we hold dear: voicing it, celebrating it and passing it on to our communities and the world, especially during difficult moments of national anguish.

I grew up in Colombia at the height of the drug wars and lived through the terrible violence there during the 1980s and early 1990s in which thousands of Colombians had been kidnapped, killed and blown up – among them members of my friends' and classmates' families. My family was fortunately spared any direct confrontation with this violence, but it hovered around our daily reality, showing itself on occasions, such as when the mafia's recruiters tried to hire our gardener and his wife, or when a cache of dynamite was found three blocks from where I was sitting in class, and most dramatically when, on a whim one day, my cousin walked down a street parallel to her usual way home and a bomb exploded on the path she usually took.

During the height of this drawn-out violence, musical performances were continuously sold out, the Philharmonic Orchestra concerts that I sang in as part of a thirty-person chorus were packed affairs, communal and art-music performances were mushrooming through the city and country as we healed our bruised psyches with the deep comfort and sonic envelopment of timpani, violins and sopranos. My family eventually left for the US when my father, the only American professor left on the faculty at the National University, was aggressively accosted by guerrilla-backed students who were angry about recent extradition laws. Soon afterwards, he was urgently warned by his own students to flee or hide.

In the ensuing years, it appeared that our life would be spared the deep anxieties of unpredictable violence. But then, in 1995, as a music student at Indiana University, while waiting backstage at the university's opera house to perform a Baroque opera, I was told by a fellow Jewish student of the fatal shooting of Israeli prime minister Yitzhak Rabin.

I also lived through the outbreak of the second intifada in Israel in 2000 while I was based at the artist residence, Mishkan Omanim in Herzliya. I was touring the performance piece *Seas of Change* about Sephardi women and exile during the terrible weeks after that fateful Rosh Hashana, when Israel and the West Bank had erupted in a wave of murders, bus bombings and rioting.

That Rosh Hashana my mother and I had been in Jerusalem. Not knowing what was brewing, we found ourselves walking through streets lined with soldiers in riot gear in East Jerusalem as we made our way to the Kotel (Wailing Wall). The next day, my former Palestinian classmate from ulpan (the Hebrew learning programme for immigrants to Israel) told me that her neighbour had died in the clashes. The following week we were horrified to see images across our TV screen of the two Israeli soldiers who were lynched for having taken a wrong turn into a Palestinian village.

The day the news of the lynching broke, we were due to perform *Seas of Change* at Mishkan Omanim. It was an excruciating decision: would a performance feel frivolous at this moment of deep national mourning? We decided to present our piece as a homage to the history of the Jewish people. After the fifty-minute performance, the audience stayed for over an hour of cathartic discussion on the horrors we had all witnessed in the previous weeks. One woman said our show had 'reminded her of the long story of exiles of the Jewish people', which she felt was crucial at this moment of bloody dispute over the land of Israel.

During the summer of 2001, I visited New York and spoke to Lynn Winters, the programming director for the Centre for Jewish History. I wanted to perform *Seas of Change* at the centre. Lynn was enthusiastic and asked me to contact her again in September, which I did. Some weeks after 9/11 she replied to tell me that their whole programming was on hold as they assessed what to do in light of the tragedy. She candidly explained that everything would change because their programming would be reacting to the catastrophe that New Yorkers had just undergone. (I eventually performed at the Centre for Jewish History in 2010 as part of the Sephardi Music Festival.)

This background is crucial in understanding the pivotal moment in which *JR* began publishing (in October 2001) and its impact on bringing the complexity of Jewish experiences to mainstream Jewish print. This essay aims to show how Sephardi Jews – whose roots stretch back to the Iberian peninsula and who often fled, after the expulsion from Spain in 1492, to live in Muslim-majority countries – and Mizrahi Jews – who are descended from local communities that existed in the Middle East and North Africa – have become a cultural bridge for a greater understanding of Muslim culture amidst the polarised global environment that ensued after 9/11 and continuing up to today.

The experience of Jews from Muslim lands has been seminal in the negotiation between the Western world and the perceived, and occasional real threat coming from Islamic radicals. You can imagine my surprise, when opening the heavy tomes of the 9/11 Commission (2005) in preparation for this essay, I found that one of the commissioners was Richard Ben-Veniste, from the Benveniste family, a Sephardi family name that has almost royal status within Ottoman Jewry.[7] Ben-Veniste, a lawyer on the Washington circuit and a presidential appointee to the Nazi War Crimes and Japanese Imperial Government Records Interagency Working Group, seemed to be continuing his historical lineage in the pursuit of the truth in painful circumstances. The hearings saw their primary task as 'to answer an essential question: What can we do to prevent another 9/11?' They saw the structural failures that had allowed this sort of event to happen to be multiple and long-reaching and

---

7   Described as an old, noble, rich and scholarly Jewish family, the Benveniste clan originate from Narbonne, France and from northern Spain from the eleventh century.

wanted to understand 'a new world in which threats develop an ocean away and strike us with horrifying impact within our own borders.'

Looking closer, it appears that Sephardi and Mizrahi Jewish culture, and music, in particular, have played an intrinsic role in the wider understanding of the Arab world during these tense decades. The Sephardi and Mizrahi world became the approachable 'other' of the Muslim world through its music and culture. The sounds and aesthetics that Jews from Muslim lands have brought to the doorstep of Europe and America have provided an approachable window into the world of the more removed Arab 'other'. Recordings, concerts, radio and television airplay, music festivals and even the merchandise that bands use to create their branding, were bringing audiences closer to what seemed to many as a remote and unknowable enemy. This music slowly brought a sonic imprint from Muslim lands in the hands of Jewish musicians, who straddle between the culture of their ancestral country (Iraq, Syria, Turkey, Yemen, Morocco) and their current cultural homes in New York, London, Los Angeles, Montreal, and Tel Aviv.

THE POST-9/11 MUSICAL WORLD

A litmus test for how much things have changed in the last twenty years can be encapsulated in my correspondence with Janusz Makuch, the director of the Jewish Culture Festival in Krakow. In the early 2000s, I sent Makuch a pitch to perform some music in Ladino (Judeo-Spanish, a language derived from medieval Spanish and originally spoken in Spain) at this iconic Polish festival. I received a short and, apparently, terse response back from him stating that they specialised in Klezmer and did not present any other Jewish musical styles. I remember replying angrily to say that they were making a grave mistake in ignoring the rest of us, and that our musical contributions were central to an understanding of the wider Jewish artistic world. In my hubris, I said something along the lines of, 'You'll see that you're making a mistake, and soon enough you'll have non-Ashkenazi music.' I have never performed there (yet!) but many of the names in the current Sephardi and Mizrahi music scene have since done so.

In 2017, the festival featured the Israeli musician Neta El Kayam, who sings Judeo-Arabic popular music from Morocco and grew up in Netivot in Israel. Netivot is also the village of the Baba Sale, the spiritual leader of Moroccan Jews. The Baba Sale represents much of what Arabic-speaking Jews in Israel are known for: a deep entrenched commitment to Jewish mysticism, lived religion and tradition, all the while accepting secular and ultra-Orthodox Jews as intrinsic parts of the larger Jewish family. The Baba Sale, whose real name is Rabbi Israel Abuhatzeira (the surname is a 'mashing up' of the words Abu Hatzeira, meaning the 'father of the carpet', which stems from a miracle story of carpet flying travel) came from the edge of the Sahara to Israel and has helped maintain a living connection to the traditions and beliefs of Jews from the Maghreb, and to the Maghreb itself. Neta and her band have in recent years done the reverse voyage, performing Moroccan repertoire in Morocco as Israelis, and surprising and moving masses of Muslim Moroccans who only recently came to know that Israeli Jews from Arab lands fiercely maintain the language, music and traditions of their ancestors.

This fluid movement of musical cultures in the years following 9/11 has also had a clear impact on how music from Muslim cultures has been received by Western society. Quite often, it has been a Jewish musician performing in Arabic, or with Muslim performers, that has opened the door to Western ears to an 'alien' or 'enemy' culture. New sounds, languages, costumes and even samples of traditional instruments began to filter through to mass audiences, who had previously ignored the nuances within Muslim cultures, creating a kind of musical public diplomacy.

At the forefront of this movement is the Israeli musician Idan Raichel, who has created what the musicologist Ilana Webster Kogan has named a simultaneous 'nationalism and cosmopolitanism' of music with his group the Idan Raichel Project. Since 2003, the band has been touring around the world, showcasing its distinctive mix of electronic music, traditional Hebrew texts and diverse influences, ranging from collaborations with traditional Yemenite vocalists to Suriname percussionists, and in languages ranging from Arabic to Aramaic. They have performed at numerous venues including New York's Central Park SummerStage, Los Angeles's Kodak Theater, the Sydney Opera House, Zenith in Paris, London's Royal Albert Hall and Vienna's Musikverein Concert Hall.

On the project's website, Idan is described as 'an ambassador representing a world of hope in which artistic collaboration breaks down barriers between people of different backgrounds and beliefs'. Audiences have been hungry for this – the band has had 262 million hits on YouTube to date. His example points to the ambassadorial potential of music and musicians, the soft power that sociologist Pierre Bourdieu writes about in his seminal book, *The Field of Cultural Production*.

It was precisely these connections that Erez Safar, the Yemenite-American music producer, was tapping into with his Sephardic Music Festival, which launched in New York's clubs in 2005. Later, in a feature in 2011 in the *New York Times*, the journalist sought to explain what Sephardi music was to mainstream readers:

As an umbrella term, Sephardic music refers loosely to the songs composed and performed by descendants or followers of Sephardi Jews, who occupied the Iberian Peninsula until their exile in the late 15th century; many resettled in

Ottoman strongholds (Turkey, Greece, Bulgaria and the Balkan lands that eventually formed Yugoslavia), parts of the Middle East and North Africa. Erez Safar, the founder and producer of the festival, said that while he often described Sephardic music as 'Jewish Middle-Eastern music,' most definitions were too narrow or too broad. Mostly, Mr Safar, whose family has roots in Yemen dating back over 2,000 years, is eager to raise awareness of Judaism's cultural diversity, which he emphasized extends beyond its 'Eastern European, Ashkenazi' face.

The first years of the festival featured a mixture of DJs, slam poets and rappers. Some of the headlining stars were established performers such as David Broza, Matisyahu and Frank London – not particularly Sephardi – but iconic in the New York Jewish, pop and radical music scene. But alongside these artists, the programme also featured a host of unquestionably Sephardi and Mizrahi artists, including Yair Dalal, Layali al-Andalus, Sarah Aroeste, as well as more experimental performers such as the Hebrew Mamita and Frantic Turtle. This eclectic curation of sounds dissolved the concept of what Jewish music was. The *Jerusalem Post* put it succinctly:

> For most New Yorkers, 'Jewish music' means klezmer: plaintive fiddles, wailing clarinets and other vestiges of a largely vanished Eastern European culture. But at the Sephardic Music Festival, a New York City tradition … the world of Jewish music gets explored from an entirely different angle, focusing on the aural legacy of Jewish communities from Spain and the Muslim world.

Time Out New York, the quintessential guide to anything creative in New York, brought this collapse of historical time into their description of Safar's festival:

> In 1492, Columbus sailed the ocean blue – and Spain and Portugal cast out their native Jews, now known as Sephardim. Some of those exiled folks picked up Balkan rhythms and Middle Eastern percussion in their new homes, adding global influence to existing Sephardic sounds. This five-day fest focuses on that musical tradition and history, with a concert that fuses Iberian staples with tango, a story slam invoking diasporic trials and dozens of international bands and solo performers reinterpreting centuries-old folk tunes.

Since Maria Rosa Menocal's 2003 book *The Ornament of the World: How Muslims, Jews and Christians Created a Culture of Tolerance in Medieval Spain*, Sephardism and what had seemed to have been lost after the expulsion of 1492, somehow was seen to hold the elusive key to what had gone wrong in the second half of the twentieth century. Could it be that the missteps by our generation contributed to bringing a group of nineteen young and educated Muslim men to destroy the heart of New York's economic life and attack the Pentagon? Menocal's book made waves and even inspired a film mixing animation with footage from southern Spain. Its publicity material said it spoke of 'a remarkable time in history when Muslims, Christians and Jews forged a common cultural identity that frequently transcended their religious differences'. The mythical *Convivencia* (the concept of a period in medieval Spain in which Jews, Muslims and Christians lived in co-existence) that was purportedly shattered with the expulsion of 1492 and the ensuing Inquisition, seemed to be a fitting frame around the current tensions of Western governments with the Muslim world.

When Safar launched the festival, one of the first synagogues he collaborated with was the historic Spanish and Portuguese Shearith Israel opposite Central Park on the Upper West Side. The congregation's Haham (Sephardi spiritual leader) was Rabbi Marc Angel, who hailed from an Ottoman Turkish and Rhodesli lineage. Having grown up in the United States, he understood that most Sephardi communities had, until the mid-twentieth century, been adept at balancing openness with tradition and were completely at home with fully participating in the wider life of the country in which they lived. His leadership in many of these matters shook the Orthodox establishment.

In 2012, during Chanukah, I was thrilled to perform in Shearith Israel's historic sanctuary for the Sephardic Music Festival. I was the only woman ever to have been granted this dispensation, after having passed a rigorous test by the Hazzan (cantor) regarding the texts of my repertoire and ensuring that I would not be dressed provocatively nor dancing during the performance. In that performance, I sang Moroccan music in Hebrew, Judeo-Arabic and Haketía (Moroccan Judeo-Spanish – a mix of medieval Spanish, Hebrew and Moroccan Arabic) and played an archival recording of one of Sami El Maghribi's praise songs to the sultan of Morocco, which was composed in 1955, upon Mohammed V's return from exile. The performance later featured in the documentary *The Wandering Muse* by Tamas Wormser.

The arc of my career has undeniably been impacted by the aftermath of 9/11. As a liberal, intellectual, left-leaning, religiously observant Sephardi woman performer and scholar, I was aware of the influence I and other musicians could wield, but I was also aware of the pitfalls of capitalising on the febrile climate that had been created by the 'War on Terror'. While I could see that some musicians such as Raichal and Safar were involved in exceptional projects, and there was also some well-meaning, honest motivation behind the sudden urge of many musicians to create peace concerts and promote interfaith work, I could not help but feel a little cynical. Often in these heavily funded inter-cultural concerts the musicians came together for rehearsals, everyone performed their bit, tensions were high as each one wanted their tradition and persona to shine, and later, everyone returned to their previous lives without any major transformation of themselves and, possibly, their audience. This was not enough for me. I wanted to understand *what* was actually happening and why and how could we learn from past lessons to impact our future.

One of these interfaith concerts in Morocco had us rehearsing at a musician's living room in Tangier, with the compulsory Jewish, Muslim and Christian singers. During the rehearsal, among the '1001-Nights' style décor of gauze curtains and 'oriental' poufs, the Arabic news programme that was showing on the room's TV flashed an image of on-duty Israeli soldiers. On top of the footage, the producers had overlaid fake blood splats. Nobody made any comment. I was dumbstruck. The seemingly tacit acceptance by the others in the room of what was obviously blatant news propaganda made what we were doing feel a charade and shattered any attempt at a peaceful interfaith musical exploration. I decided the only way to really move forward was to be involved in longstanding educational collaborations involving depth and understanding rather than one-off shared performances between parties of 'different' camps. This was what propelled me to embark on a study of Moroccan Jewish music and poetry (supported by a Senior Fulbright Research grant) in 2007. I was fascinated by the Jewish community in Tangier, which has maintained its delicate balance of belonging to a unique community and individuation from an overwhelming Muslim majority. Music is at the heart of their core identity and the feeling of belonging to the general population while simultaneously being an eternal 'foreigner', is navigated elegantly on a daily basis.

A decade later, I found myself a researcher at the oldest music faculty in the world, in Cambridge. The college I am affiliated to, Peterhouse, is built on land that belonged to a Jewish merchant before the expulsion of the Jews from England. These historic confluences that sit on the earth beneath me make me wonder if the Jews from Muslim countries understood something about the delicate balancing between being a Jewish minority within an occasionally hostile, non-Jewish majority that we can continue to learn from today. Or maybe it was the Muslim majority that understood for centuries how to incorporate the Jewish minority into their societies by living side by side but not overly mixing with them? As the Tangier Jewish writer Rachel Muyal put it to me ten years ago: '*juntos pero no revueltos*' — together but not scrambled.

HISTORIC BOUNDARY-CROSSERS

The very concept of being a boundary-crosser or, in Hebrew, an 'Ivri', is foundational to Judaism. Jewish theology can serve as a framework to analyse how traces left by music demonstrate how Jewish composers, performers and community leaders interacted with local and transnational political events. The deployment of certain melodies and musical styles over others within the Jewish community and the interaction of artists, clergy and other community stakeholders with political infrastructures throughout history, point to an encoded dialogue between Jewish cultural production and official cultural tropes. In Hebrew, the ancient two-letter root for 'Ivri'– 'v' and 'r' – is the same as that for the word 'overe' (to cross) and for the name of the first Jewish patriarch, Avraham, who founded the Jewish people when he 'crossed' over from idolatry to monotheism.

Jewish philosophy deems that the concept of crossing boundaries is inscribed into the societal and cultural body of the Jew. The weekly Torah portion that tells the story of Avraham as the creator of monotheism is entitled *Lech lecha,* which some translate as go 'unto' yourself. Avram, his original name, was written without the letter 'hey', which symbolises God. Avram was told by God to travel away from his land, people and family to a new land in order to become the patriarch of a great nation (Genesis 12: 1–3). Only after detaching from his previous life was his name changed from Avram to Avraham, thus including the 'h' of God's name within his very name.

When thinking of the creativity that often emerges from those who 'cross' communal divides, it is significant that the very first notation of a Jewish musical piece was done by a convert to Judaism. The twelfth-century Obadiah the Proselyte (ha-Ger) had been an Italian monk and converted to Judaism. His monastic education included the Lombardic neumatic system for musical notation used for Gregorian chant. After his conversion to Judaism, he travelled to Syria, Palestine and Baghdad, where he mastered Hebrew script and, thus, the musical notations in his hand found in the Cairo Geniza have Italian musical notation and Eastern Hebrew script - an uncommon combination which had puzzled scholars until recently.

Obadiah eventually settled in Egypt, joining its dynamic Jewish community. His 'crossing' over into Judaism provides us with the earliest notated melodies that can safely be assumed to have been used by Jews. The liturgical and paraliturgical chants 'Mi al Har Horev', 'Baruch HaGever' and 'Wa Eda-Mah' were brought to light in 1918 from fragments from the Cairo Geniza. However, because of their obscure origins and recent discovery, these melodies have remained virtually unknown. From the 1970s, the Israeli composer Andre Hajdu arranged these three melodies for voice and piano and occasionally the solo vocal chants appear on medieval recordings, but other than that they are almost forgotten.

Four centuries later, another example of a musical Jew 'crossing' genres is also an Italian. Salomone Rossi (1570–1630) was a violinist and composer and a transitional figure between the late Italian Renaissance period and early Baroque.

He was the concertmaster at the Gonzaga court in Mantua during a period of heightened antisemitism, but because of his favour in court was exempted from wearing the yellow badge that had to be worn by other Jews. After writing Italian vocal and instrumental music for decades, Rossi wrote a volume of Jewish sacred music (1623), considered to be the first collection of originally composed music for Hebrew psalms and prayers. Leon of Modena (1571–1648), a friend of Rossi's, justified polyphonic practice in services and celebrations in his essays. Italian rabbis may have been influenced by Rossi when they issued a letter in 1605 authorising the introduction of polyphonic music with notes of fixed rhythmic value into the synagogue.

During this period, a large influx of Sephardi intellectuals had arrived in Italy from the Iberian Peninsula after the traumatic expulsion of Jews from Spain in 1492. In Italian intellectual circles a rich discussion about music, Kabbalah (Jewish mysticism) and agency ensued. Around 1560, a mere fifty-eight years after the expulsion from Spain, the books *Sefer Heshek Shelomo* (*The Book of Solomon's Desire*), an interpretation of Song of Songs written by Yohanan Alemano, and *Nigun HaOlam* (*Melody of the World*), a philosophical treatise about the power of man to create cosmic harmony by Isaac Arama, were published. These were written soon after Marsilio Ficino's publications in Florence on music and magic where Ficino expounded on neo-Platonic concepts of music, mathematics, astronomy and health.

Entangling the narrative even more, Leon of Modena, who served as cantor in the synagogue of Ferrara, was vocally opposed to Kabbalah, calling it an invented tradition. But as Eric Hobsbawm and Terence Ranger wrote in *The Invention of Tradition* (1992), traditions are *often* created and propelled to cement the identity of a group. I believe that for post-expulsion exiles these kabbalistic texts of how the world, which appeared to have crumbled around them, could be changed through their thoughts, voices and actions carried a very comforting message of agency and impact.

These writers were wrestling with the Divine, like Jacob the patriarch's biblical wrestling with the angels. After the cataclysm of the expulsion and as they wrestled and crossed into a new land, these writers, philosophers and musicians tried to find a way to enable music to act as a theurgic tool for humans to make an impact on the world.

The biblical narrative that was most notable in these explorations was the story of Jacob, who fought with the angel of death by the edge of a river and was able to *cross over* after not giving up, winning him the name of Israel – he who wrestles with God. Wrestling takes the form of questioning the status quo and pushing for change. Jacob became the founding father of the twelve tribes of Israel, who were not only Hebrews, boundary crossers, but Israelites, those who wrestle with God, those who question. These two elements, boundary crosser and questioner, recur throughout the relationship between Sephardim, the Muslim world and Europe. It is significant that in Sephardi musical repertoire, it is the song 'Abraham Avinu' that is recognised and sung across the world, thus linking Sephardi identity to the monotheism of Muslims and Christians who also consider Avraham their ancestor.

In the Hebrew language books on music of the Italian Renaissance, the authors approached music through the sephirotic tree (also known as 'the tree of life', a central symbol of Kabbalah) and its capacity to draw down the divine power through song to impact the world through focused singing. By using Hebrew and not the vernacular, they were writing for an audience familiar with rabbinic texts while drawing from neo-Platonic philosophy and connecting Jewish music to science and astronomical movements.

FROM THE VENICE GHETTO TO GEORGE GERSHWIN

The connection of music to power was inscribed into Kabbalistic theory by sixteenth-century writers and philosophers such as Isaac Abarbanel, Meir ibn Gabbay, Shelomo Alkabetz and Moshe Cordovero and particularly in the work of Chaim Vital (1542–1620) in his book *Etz Haim* (*Tree of Life*). These post-expulsion texts of music and mysticism thus granted agency to every Jew to affect the supernal and created world through their voices. At a time when so many people must have felt despair at seeing the Sephardi world disappear, this renewed sense of personal agency must have provided solace to many. These traces of the interacting agency between sung liturgy and Kabbalistic theurgy were still present in prayerbooks from Tangier as late as the early twenty-first century, as I found in discussions with current members of the community between 2007 and 2011.

Non-Jewish musicians have long been interested in Jewish traditional music. A hundred years after Rossi, the Catholic composer Benedetto Marcello (1686–1739) 'crossed' into the Venetian Ghetto and gathered ten melodies from the Sephardi liturgy for his *Estro Poetico-Armonico: Parafrasi Sopra Salmi*. Marcello's settings of Jewish melodies and the publication of those melodies in Hebrew in his larger compendium of psalm compositions brought a portion of Venetian synagogue music into the wider world. In the nineteenth century the Salmi were translated into many other languages, including French, German, Swedish, English and Russian.

The fact that some cantors from the Venice Ghetto shared their melodies with Marcello meant that for the first time, various generations of non-Jewish musicians had access to synagogue melodies and some of them began to permeate vocal and instrumental music performances. This movement of liturgical and religo-specific music into the non-Jewish public sphere began a two-century process that culminated with the German composer Max Bruch's 'Kol Nidrei' and its performance for the epitome of anti-Jewish audiences, Nazi officials at Auschwitz. Bruch completed his 'Kol Nidrei' in Liverpool in 1880 and published it in Berlin in 1881. He, however, said himself that he was a Protestant and did not compose Jewish music, but was only inspired by Jewish 'folk' melodies.

Which brings us to the question: what is Jewish music? Is it 'folk' melodies, connected to liturgy or Jewish vernacular languages, or is Jewish music an expression of a certain life-experience that might be similar to any Jewish experience around the world? Maybe it is the sounding out of that simultaneous belonging and non-belonging that sits at the heart of Jewish musical expression? This question is particularly relevant in our fast-paced, increasingly connected world, where cultural specificities seem to hold on tenaciously in the face of mass popular culture and social media.

In the post-Enlightenment generations in the West, Jewish musicians entered classical music's mainstream. As many Jews became secular, abolishing externally identifiable differences with their surrounding culture, more Jewish artists appeared on the concert stage and Jewish audiences increased too.

Some of these artists kept an active link to their 'Jewish' musical identities, drawing on songs in Jewish vernacular languages or liturgical and paraliturgical songs. The most famous example of this is in the compositions of George Gershwin, where Gershwin used synagogue modes in his melodies, which in turn became part of wider popular culture.

However, the drive for gathering and classifying folk melodies continued. In early twentieth-century Madrid, Spanish philologists such as Ramón Menéndez Pidal and Tomás Navarro Tomás were busy recording Judeo-Spanish songs as proof of Spain's ownership of the cultural capital of Jews throughout the Mediterranean basin. They harkened back to the work of Johann Gottfried Herder, who coined the word *Volkslied* (folk song) in the 1770s and who first linked the idea of folk melodies and the building of national identities. The work of these Spanish philologists brought Sephardi repertoire to the compositional mainstream, inspiring intellectuals such as Federico García Lorca and later Joaquín Díaz to set songs and perform them as part of Spain's historic musical heritage.

'AVRAHAM AVINU' – THE SEPHARDI GLOBAL HIT

The story of the song 'Avraham Avinu' (Abraham our Father), the paean of Sephardi Jews, epitomises the wider embrace of Sephardi music in the early decades of the twentieth century. The song became famous after it was a hit for the Israeli musician Yehoram Gaon in 1969. In recent years, its popularity on YouTube has further cemented it as the self-proclaimed anthem of Sephardi Jews.

The arrangement that Gaon used in his hit song was actually created in 1937 by Wolf Simoni (later known as Louis Saguer). Simoni was a German Jewish refugee who was living in Paris when he wrote the piece. To complicate matters, the original text of this song can be found in a manuscript originating in eighteenth-century Bosnia (which has been researched by the leading Spanish philologist Elena Romero from the Consejo Superior de Investigaciones Científicas, Spain's national research institute). But the exact origin of the melody remains unidentified. Ethnomusicologist Edwin Seroussi, who has written extensively about the origin of this piece, has concluded that it probably hails from northern Morocco's Jewish communities, and may be a zarzuela melody (the zarzuela is a dramatic genre that alternates between spoken and sung scenes) that came across the Straits of Gibraltar with the Spanish protectorate's cultural diplomacy efforts in the early part of the twentieth century.

There are many further layers to the story behind 'Avraham Avinu'. Simoni moved to Paris from Berlin in 1929 and studied composition with Arthur Honneger (1892–1955) and Darius Milhaud (1892–1974). His arrangement of 'Avraham Avinu' was the fourth song of a set of four Sephardi art songs and he dedicated it to the young Spanish composer Gustavo Durán Martínez. Durán had lived in Paris immediately after his years at the Residencia de Estudiantes, an elite campus for arts students in Madrid, where he had studied composition. He was a member of Spain's Generación del 27 (an influential group of Spanish poets) and had been friends with Lorca, Salvador Dalí, Luis Buñuel and Rafael Alberti. In the 1920s, he had composed four romances in Judeo-Spanish (called *Romances Castellanos de los Balcanes*) for voice and piano, each embodying one Sephardi city: Salonica, Sofia, Belgrade and Constantinople. The musical gaze toward Sephardi cities by a young composer from the Generación del 27 demonstrates the breadth of influence of the musical philosephardi movement that had been launched by Menéndez Pidal's project years before.

However, by the time Simoni published his arrangement of 'Avraham Avinu', Durán had abandoned composition and was enlisted in the Republican army to fight Franco's fascism and later became a commander, leading his brigade into the Battle of Coruña Road and the Segovia offensive. During the mid 1930s, Sephardi fascist resistance was denounced in the media. One of the first to be publicly accused was Dr Alberto Bandelac de Pariente, the physician for the Spanish embassy in Paris, who came from an eminent Tangier Sephardi family and was the founder of the Asociación Hispano-Hebrea (the Spanish-Hebrew Association). In 1936 he was accused by the pro-Falange, anti-Mason and antisemite Mauricio Carlavilla of having poisoned the dictator and former Spanish prime minister Primo de Rivera, who died suddenly as he was leaving Paris to live in exile in Germany in 1930. After the accusation and public scandal, Bandelac de Pariente's reputation was demolished and he is believed to have been murdered in 1942, at the height of Vichy tensions in Paris.

It is fascinating to summarise the journey of 'Avraham Avinu': it began as a Bosnian Judeo-Spanish text with a late nineteenth-century zarzuela melody that was probably taken from northern Morocco to Spain. It then became known to a German-Jewish refugee in Paris, who notated, arranged and published it and dedicated it to a Spanish military man who was commanding battles against fascism at the time of publication. To cap it all, Duran is a Spanish-Jewish family name, meaning that our Spanish composer and soldier, who went on to become a political strategist for the FBI and eventually a representative to the United Nations, could have been a descendant of crypto-Jews. The anthem embodies the Sephardi concept of Ivri and is one example in a long chain of Jewish music traversing international politics and events as a beacon of sonic intervention, blending differences and singing the hope and pain of the generation it hails from.

SEEDS OF CHANGE

The fantastically successful trajectory of the Idan Raichel Project, mentioned above, embodies a very multilingual and transnational musical story – performing in Arabic, German, Spanish, Amharic, French and Hebrew to multilingual audiences internationally. This multiplicity of cultures, languages and musical expression breaks at the idea of any single 'pure' Jewish sound. Jewish sound might just be any sound that reminds us of our constant mobility and layered cultures. And keeping this in mind is useful as an antidote to the idea that Jewish music is represented by the sounds of Tin Pan Alley, Yiddish theatre, American musical theatre or Hollywood – all of which brought elements of Ashkenazi musical aesthetics to world audiences.

My vantage point as a Western Sephardi Jewish scholar of the music connected to al-Andalus (the region under Muslim rule on the Iberian peninsula from the sixth to the fifteenth century) and its diasporas and with connections to the United States, Israel, Morocco, Colombia and the UK tells me that these historical connections between cultures, languages, music and places have made Jewish music – especially Sephardi and Mizrahi music – central to the opening of closed minds over the last twenty years. Sephardim have been cosmopolitan for generations, thanks to their trade networks throughout the Mediterranean, intellectual exchange from medieval Baghdad to Cairo, Fez, Constantinople, Leghorn and Córdoba and the forced and chosen migrations of families in the nineteenth and twentieth centuries to India, Hong Kong, Zimbabwe, Venezuela and the Brazilian Amazon, placing capillaries of Jewish experience and contacts in often remote and unexpected locales. Other more seemingly straightforward connections have provided no less of a seminal musical influence such as those between London, Amsterdam and New York. For example, stemming from the musical relationship between the anglophone Western Sephardi congregations of Bevis Marks in London and Shearith Israel in Manhattan, London and New York's Jewish communities have had a musical backbone connecting them, not just through the popular music circuit, but also through the back alleys of liturgy and ancestral religious musicking.

Which takes us back to Safar and his Sephardi music festival project in New York. Recently, in addition to the festival, Safar has created 'The Semitic' clothing label on his Shemspeed production label, where, cheekily, his sampled sounds seem to have spilled over into sampled clothing, including Jewish keffiyehs named *Am Yisrael Hai*, covered with Stars of David and in 2020, face-masks with Stars of David incorporated into a check pattern that could be mistaken as a keffiyeh fabric from afar. His website brings all of this together. It reads:

> Shemspeed is an independent recording label and promotional agency highlight-ing cross-over music artists with positive and unifying messages ... Shemspeed artists, collectively showcasing the diversity in world Jewish music, have performed with musicians as varied as Snoop Dogg, Lou Reed, Idan Raichel and Eminem ... Shemspeed's mission is unifying people through culture and education, celebrat-ing diversity and common ground. By way of this work, we add a public Jewish voice to multi-cultural, inter-faith, creative and collaborative bridge-building.

The very bridge-building that Obadiah, Rossi and others have strived to build for centuries.

In London, this ethos is also evident. Since 2011 Jennifer Jankel, the daughter of bandleader Joe Loss, has been the chair of the Board of Trustees of the Jewish Music Institute (JMI) in London. The JMI supports Jewish musical creativity and perfor-mance in projects spanning from education to concerts, festivals, compositions and avant-garde events. Jankel has continued her father's deep commitment to a Jewish identity, which he maintained while succeeding as a wildly successful mainstream performer (appearing at Queen Elizabeth II's 50th birthday party and at the Queen Mother's 80th celebrations). On its website, JMI states that its mission is 'bringing Jewish music to the mainstream British and international cultural arena'. In recent years, the JMI has underwritten or supported two major projects of music from Jews from Muslim lands.

The first, *The Wolf of Baghdad*, which premiered in 2017, was created by Carol Isaacs (also known as cartoonist The Surreal McCoy), with the Judeo-Arabic ensemble 3yin. This audio-visual project traces Isaac's Iraqi-Jewish family's memories of their lost homeland, bringing together a variety of London-based Jewish musicians from Sephardi groups: Los Desterrados, Rivers of Babylon, Baladi Blues, Hamsa and the London Klezmer Quartet. This was a true bridging of the Sephardi, Mizrahi and Ashkenazi Jewish music continuum. By 2019, *The Wolf of Baghdad* had screened to a full house at the London Jewish Film Festival and in January 2020, London's Cartoon Museum hosted the launch of Isaac's graphic novel of the same name.

A short month before the Covid-19 pandemic shutdowns in early 2020, JMI launched Yallah: Judeo-Arabic Music Conference and Workshop, which I had helped initiate as a recent JMI Trustee (and for which *JR* was a media partner). At the event we were honoured to welcome the Jewish advisor to the king of Morocco, André Azoulay, and the Moroccan ambassador to the UK, Abdesselam Aboudrar. During the opening concert on 9 February (featuring Haim Botbol, Morocco's Jewish Frank Sinatra), Ambassador Aboudrar stated:

> [Music is] … to the minds, the hearts, the senses, a universal language. But it is not only about universality, but also identity, but not the kind of pathological identity we are facing now throughout the world, it is the bright side of identity. Which means, it is not about us versus them, but it is about what can *we* bring to the others. And this is very important.

That evening a standing-room-only audience of Londoners – Jewish, Christian and Muslim – clapped, danced and sang to the infectious rhythms of a Jew performing popular music in Arabic.

Does, then, the issue of a music's Jewishness rest on issues of reception and the perception of those who hear it? I do believe that the issue of reception is of primordial importance. It casts a light on questions such as how listeners and audiences perceive and engage with music that is packaged as Jewish. The deeper question is: do listeners react to music differently depending on the label it comes with? If mainstream media thought of Leonard Cohen, Bob Dylan or Amy Winehouse as performing Jewish music, would its relevance for the wider society be questioned? Possibly.

In the last twenty years, since the launch of *JR* and the aftermath of 9/11, cultural organisations that promote the creativity of Jewish artists, be they musicians, writers, filmmakers or visual artists, have cast their gaze more deliberately on Sephardi and Mizrahi artists. Learning about culture from Muslim lands, through a Jewish lens, has provided audiences with a route through which they can become more familiar and understand Muslim culture. Mainstream media is accustomed to Jewish celebrities, many having inhabited people's experiences of the stage, silver screen and TV during the twentieth century. Just as during pre-Enlightenment times, when Jewish diplomats travelled between Christian and Muslim courts, the Jewish musician has been the diplomatic go-between providing an interface – as a member of both cultures and not fully belonging to either.

In this two-decade span, *JR* has continually covered stories on Jews from Muslim countries, including special reports from Iraq (2001), Egypt (2003), Morocco (2006), Ethiopia (2007), Turkey (2010, 2019) and Uzbekistan (2013). I was thrilled to see that in the very first issue of *JR* in October 2001, the great Yeheskel Kohaman, an Iraqi Jewish performer who lived in London until his recent death, had written an article on the Jewish contribution to Iraqi music. Ten years later, the magazine reflected the growing conversation around the place of women in popular Jewish music by featuring on the cover of its April 2011 issue the Iranian-American singer Galit Dardashti. With a darbuka (traditional drum) in her arm and a sleeveless black dress hugging her advanced baby bump, she cut a dramatic figure. The January 2016 magazine featured Yemenite-Israeli sisters A-Wa, in full traditional garb, as they promoted their groundbreaking mix of traditional sounds, rap music and striking visual iconography to a mainstream audience. A-Wa's following is strong amongst the Yemenite Muslim youth because they embody a freedom for young women that is seen as inspirational. They are making a sonic bridge between Western audiences and young Muslims in the Arab countries from the Gulf. The April 2021 issue of *JR* featured a portrait of the Israeli-Persian musician Liraz, striking in a bright pink blazer and bold blue eye shadow, whose work with musicians based in Iran draws on her family's heritage.

Other features have included an interview with Iraqi-Israeli musician Yair Dalal (2017), coverage of the JMI Yallah conference (2020) and a piece by the veteran Middle East correspondent Ian Black about the Abraham Accords (2020), the recent political rapprochement between Israel and the Gulf states. Since 2016, the magazine has also run a whole new section called 'Sephardi Renaissance', which has featured culture across the Sephardi world, including books, food, art and film. Might Jewish readers be more open to this simply because of the twenty-year-old educational process through Jewish music (and cuisine) that has flourished since the difficult years between September 2001 and today?

Jewish musical bridge-building has been around for at least a millennium, since Obadiah wrote down those Hebrew melodies in medieval Christian neumatic notation through to Salomone Rossi, Felix Mendelssohn, Arnold Schoenberg, Amy Winehouse and Idan Raichel. Over the last twenty years, those border-crossers have often been the rhythms, music and aesthetics of the Sephardi and Mizrahi world, which have brought the Muslim, Christian and Jewish worlds closer and helped audiences understand (and come to love) what others might deem to be too threatening to engage with.

As I write these concluding words on the Fast of Esther in 2021 (the fast traditionally held before the festival of Purim), on the other side of a year of shutdowns and restrictions because of the Covid-19 pandemic, I think of Esther, that Persian Mizrahi queen. I think of how she demonstrated that having the courage to fully belong to seemingly opposing worlds simultaneously was the position which, in the end, was the only one poised to bring redemption to all. What will the next twenty years post-pandemic bring through the Jewish culture broker? The seeds are already germinating.

APPENDIX 1: BIBLIOGRAPHY

Bohlman, Philip V., *Jewish Music and Modernity* (Oxford: Oxford University Press, 2008)

Bohlman, Philip V., 'Johann Gottfried Herder and the Global Moment of World-Music History', in *The Cambridge History of World Music*, ed. Philip V. Bohlman (Cambridge: Cambridge University Press, 2013), pp. 255–76

George Bozarth, 'Salomone Rossi, A Transitional Figure'

Bronner, Simon (ed.), *Framing Jewish Culture: Boundaries and Representations* (Oxford: The Littman Library of Jewish Civilization, 2014)

Conway, David, *Jewry in Music: Entry to the Profession from the Enlightenment to Richard Wagner* (Cambridge: Cambridge University Press, 2012)

Elbaz, Vanessa Paloma, 'Jewish Music in Northern Morocco and the Building of Sonic Identity Boundaries', *The Journal of North African Studies* (2021), DOI: 10.1080/13629387.2021.1884855

Elbaz, Vanessa Paloma, 'Judeo-Spanish Melodies in the Liturgy of Tangier: Feminine Imprints in a Masculine Space' in Ruth Davis (ed.), *Musical Exodus: Al-Andalus and its Jewish Diasporas* (Lanham: Rowman & Littlefield, 2015), pp. 25–43

Fifield, Christopher, *Max Bruch: His Life and Works* (Woodbridge: Boydell Press, 2005)

Glasser, Jonathan, *The Lost Paradise: Andalusi Music in Urban North Africa* (Chicago: University of Chicago Press, 2016)

Glenn, Susan A. and Sokoloff, Naomi B. (eds.), *Boundaries of Jewish Identity* (Seattle: University of Washington Press, 2010)

Harran, Don, 'The Hebrew Exemplum as a Force of Renewal in 18th-Century

Musical Thought: The Case of Benedetto Marcello and His Collection of Psalms', in Andreas Geiger and Thomas J. Mathiesen (eds), *Music in the Mirror: Reflections on the History of Music Theory and Literature for the 21st Century* (Lincoln: University of Nebraska Press, 2002), pp. 143–94

Hobsbawm, Eric and Ranger, Terry O., *The Invention of Tradition* (Cambridge: Cambridge University Press, 1992)

Holbein, James R., *The 9/11 Commission: Proceedings and Analysis Books 1–2* (New York: Oceana Publications, 2005)

Idel, Moshe, 'Conceptualizations of Music in Jewish Mysticism,' in Lawrence Sullivan (ed.), *Enchanting Powers, Music in the World's Religions* (Cambridge: Harvard University Press, 1997), pp. 159–88

Idel, Moshe, 'Anamnesis and Music, or Kabbalah as Renaissance before the Renaissance', in *Rivista di Storia e Litteratura Religiosa, 2* (Florence: ed. Leo S. Olschki, 2013), pp. 389–412.

Romero, Elena, 'Formas estróficas de las coplas sefardíes', in F. Corriente and Á. Sáenz-Badillos (eds.), *Poesía estrófica, Actas del primer congreso internacional sobre poesía estrófica árabe y hebrea y sus paralelos romances* (Madrid: Universidad Complutense et alii, 1991), pp. 259–78.

Selfridge-Field, Eleanor, 'Marcello, Benedetto Giacomo,' in Stanley Sadie and John Tyrrel (eds.), *The New Grove Dictionary of Music and Musicians*, rev. ed. (London: Oxford University Press, 2001), vol. 15, pp. 809–12.

Seroussi, Edwin, *Ruinas Sonoras de la modernidad: La cancion popular sefardí en la era post-tradicional* (Madrid: Consejo Superior de Investigaciones Científicas, 2019)

Seroussi, Edwin, 'In Search of Jewish Musical Antiquity in the 18th-Century Venetian Ghetto: Reconsidering the Hebrew Melodies in Benedetto Marcello's "Estro Poetico-Armonico"', *The Jewish Quarterly Review*, vol. 93, no. 1/2 (2002), 149–99

Shannon, Jonathan, *Performing al-Andalus: Music and Nostalgia across the Mediterranean* (Bloomington: Indiana University Press, 2015)

Summit, Jeffrey A., '"I'm a Yankee Doodle Dandy"? Identity and Melody at an American Simhat Torah Celebration', *Ethnomusicology*, vol. 37, no. 1 (1993), 41–62

Voss, Angela, 'The Natural Magic of Marsilio Ficino', *Historical Dance*, vol. 3, no. 1 (1992), 25–30, https://earlymusicseattle.org/salomone-rossi-a-transitional-figure/

'JEWS AND BLACK MUSIC: A DIFFICULT RELATIONSHIP', BY KEITH KAHN-HARRIS

In the April 2004 issue of JR*, Keith Kahn-Harris explored how the relationship between Jews and black music illuminates issues of assimilation and confidence experienced in wider society by each of these minority groups.*

Keith Kahn-Harris is a senior lecturer at Leo Baeck College, an associate lecturer at Birkbeck College, and an associate fellow of the Institute for Jewish Policy Research. His publications include Extreme Metal: Music and Culture on the Edge *(Berg, 2007) and* Turbulent Times: The British Jewish Community Today *(with Ben Gidley – Continuum, 2012).*

In 1995, Rabbi Michael Lerner, editor of *Tikkun* magazine, together with the African-American philosopher Cornell West published a book entitled *Jews and Blacks: Let the Healing Begin.* The title says much about the woeful relations between black people and Jews (in the USA at least). In recent decades, Jewish and black communities have been separated by a cavernous social distance, living in different areas and inhabiting different social classes. Whereas Jews appear to represent the possibilities of post-war assimilation and a comfortable accommodation with western culture, the black community appears to represent the discomforts of racism and alienation. Jewish and black people not only live separate lives; they are suspicious of each other's way of being a minority.

But there is an alternative narrative of Jewish-black relations that tells a story of much closer, although still problematic, relations. In the sphere of popular music, the destinies of Jews and black people have been much more closely intertwined.

Marginal groups, denied the possibility of cultural expression through 'official' channels, have traditionally looked to the field of popular culture to make their mark. As far back as the 19th century, black American musicians were hugely popular as 'minstrels' in a highly racist society. When Jews began arriving in large numbers in America from Eastern Europe in the late 19th century, they also looked to the entertainment business to make their fortunes and find a degree of acceptance in a hostile world.

But whereas the music associated with black musicians was and remains irrevocably associated with their 'blackness', Jewish musicians, on the whole, made every effort to avoid drawing attention to their Jewishness, changing their names and, with some important exceptions, largely avoiding any kind of Jewish repertoire. So there is something odd about the Jewish presence in popular music: Jews have been ubiquitous, yet references to Jewishness and to Judaism have been rare.

That is not to say that the Jewishness of Jewish songwriters, performers and impresarios was and is of no consequence to their work. On the contrary, it is crucial to understanding the work of many key Jewish figures in the entertainment industry. Yet Jewishness is expressed covertly and indirectly and one of these indirect ways through which Jewishness has been expressed is through Jews' use of and relationship to black cultural forms.

Take the example of 'blackface' performance, which is the use of make-up by white artists to imitate blackness. Although Jews didn't invent blackface, by the early 20th century, Jews had become its principal exponents. Such significant figures as Edie Cantor, Sophie Tucker and – most famously of all – Al Jolson, all started off as blackface performers.

Today blackface appears to us as grotesquely racist. A simple-minded figure munching watermelon and waxing lyrical about 'swanee', 'dixie' and 'mammy', is not merely dated but offensive. As a result the work of contemporary cultural historians has been required to tease out some of the complexities of the art form. What such work has shown is that the Jewish use of blackface was not a result of simple racism but something much more complex.

In the early 20th century, Jews were in a much less comfortable social position than they are today. Facing racism and poverty, they nonetheless fought hard to gain upward mobility through the social system. Yet even as they did so, many felt ambivalent about their increasing social status and in particular about the assimilation and compromises required of them. The idea of the 'melting pot' – so treasured by many Jews – also brought with it a loss of Jewish identity. Most strikingly, it required that Jews become seen as, and identify as 'white', since 'whiteness' conferred the only route to status in a society in which marginality and blackness was despised.

The historian Michael Alexander explains that 'as Jews moved up they identified down'. They retained an attraction for the perhaps more 'truthful' world from which they had come – the world of the despised, 'low' other. To retain this attraction when Jews were moving up the social scale and striving for respectability created a quandary that blackface helped to solve. By donning the trappings of blackness, Jews could participate in the jazz age whilst still retaining the benefits of Jewish upward mobility.

So although blackface drew on a grotesque travesty of 'actual' black culture, it was less a manifestation of Jewish racism than of the desire of some Jews for a more 'authentic' form of existence. This helps us to understand the famous final scene in Al Jolson's *The Jazz Singer* a little better. When Jolson sings with such feeling for his 'Mammy' he is at once, as a successful jazz singer, proclaiming the unbridgeable distance to his roots (symbolised by the mother figure) and at the same time, through taking on the mask of blackness, showing that part of him will always remain as the marginal Jewish outsider.

Blackface is only the most extreme case depicting Jewish attraction towards and repulsion from both black and white society. At times, Jewish use of black culture and black music has revealed an uncomfortable tendency to appropriate and exploit. Take George Gershwin, whose works such as 'Rhapsody in Blue' and of course 'Porgy and Bess' are celebrated as triumphs of the jazz age. Gershwin has been revered for his ear for black music and his diligent research amongst the black community. So perfect does Gershwin's work appear as a distillation of all that is great in black music, that it virtually dispenses with the need for black composers at all. Indeed, in the context of the 1930s, Gershwin and other Jewish masters of black music neatly solved a tricky problem for white people – black music was attractive but black people themselves were not. Whilst Gershwin himself was immensely sympathetic to black culture and whilst his music is still revered by many African-Americans, his success did nothing to help the low status of black composers in the music industry.

This is then the irony: that however much Jews have opposed racism, for much of the 20th century Jews occupied a position in American culture – not so marginal to suffer overmuch from racism, yet marginal enough to provide useful cultural 'middle men' to those who truly were on the margins. This helped to perpetuate the low status of African-Americans even as it popularised black music.

In his book, *Rock 'n' Roll Jews*, Michael Billig argues that Jews played a crucial role in the creation of rock and roll by acting as cultural intermediaries between the black and white worlds. Jews only had a limited involvement in rock and roll as performers, but in the 1950s and 1960s they were heavily involved as writers, producers and impresarios: figures such as Allan Freed (the DJ who coined the term 'rock and roll'), Leiber and Stoller (who wrote Elvis Presley's 'Hound Dog') and the legendary producer Phil Spector. Such figures grew up in modest circumstances at a time when Jews lived near black areas and where there was a relatively consistent level of social interaction between Jewish and black people.

Their ability to 'pass' as white made being successful in the music and entertainment industries easier than such success was for black musicians.

By the 1960s and 1970s, Jews' social position had changed, and most of the community had taken on all the privileges of middle-class white society. The flight out of black inner-city areas meant that Jews had much less contact with black people. At the same time, the civil rights and black power movements had led to a growing confidence and self-assertion in the black community. No longer willing to trust their cultural future to white or Jewish intermediaries, black writers, producers and entrepreneurs took on growing importance – this was the era of Motown and James Brown. Jews no longer had any need or ability to express themselves through reworkings of black music and black performers were increasingly reluctant to let themselves be appropriated in this way.

Jews have remained in large numbers in the entertainment industry, still more likely to be writers, producers and impresarios rather than performers. But it has become less easy to identify a distinctly Jewish contribution to the content of popular music and culture. Rapidly assimilating but still nonetheless marginal, Jews in the jazz age and beyond had looked to black music and black culture as a way of expressing their ambivalence and excitement about becoming Americans. Jews bought up in the comfortable 1970s and beyond, whilst they inherited the drive to make it in the entertainment industries, were much less driven to express themselves in a distinctive way. It is as though once Jews lost the desire and ability to express themselves through their relationship to black culture, they lost their ability to express themselves in a distinctive way at all in popular music.

At the start of the 21st century, Jews find themselves – for all their success and ubiquity in the entertainment industries – almost culturally invisible in musical terms. This invisibility is all the more striking when compared to the vibrancy of black music. It also contrasts significantly with the Jews' contribution to literature, theatre, cinema and 'non-popular' musics. But there are signs that this situation may be changing. A growing number of artists are mixing traditional Jewish musical styles with other popular forms. In the UK, for example, Oi Va Voi serve up an intoxicating brew of klezmer and dance music. There are even Jewish rap and hip-hop acts, such as Hip Hop Hoodios, that are trying – if a little uncertainly – to create a more substantial Jewish engagement with black music than has been attempted in the past. The current upsurge in interest in Jewish culture is motivated by a desire to express Jewishness in a distinctive way. Perhaps the time has come for Jews to come out from behind the scenes and emerge as musicians and performers in their own right. Perhaps in the 20th century, relations between Jewish and black musicians will become relations between equals.

SELECTED BIBLIOGRAPHY

Michael Alexander (2001), *Jazz Age Jews*, Princeton University Press

Michael Billig (2000), *Rock 'n' Roll Jews*, Five Leaves Publications: London

Michael Lerner and Cornell West (1995), *Jews and Blacks: Let the Healing Begin*, Putnam Press

Jeffrey Melnick (2001), *A Right to Sing the Blues: African Americans, Jews and American Popular Song*, Harvard University Press

Michael Rogin (1996), *Blackface. White Noise: Jewish Immigrants in the Melting Pot*, University of California Press

FROM THE *JR* ARCHIVE

'SAY YES! TO YEMENITE FOLK', BY DANIELLE GOLDSTEIN

A-Wa, a trio of Yemenite sisters, were the stars on the front cover of JR*'s January 2016 issue. In this interview with the eldest sister, Tair Haim, Danielle Goldstein uncovered how the band, who hail from an Israeli desert town, are at the forefront of a Yemini-Arabic folk music comeback.*

Danielle Goldstein is JR*'s associate editor and content manager. She is the powerhouse behind the magazine's music and listings sections, as well as editing* JR*'s website, newsletter, blog and social channels. She also fronts the indie band Collars.*

In the southern tip of Israel lies Shaharut, a small settlement surrounded by sand, rocks and mountainous terrain. Just over a hundred families live there, but one in particular is causing a stir right now: the Haim sisters. These three young women – 32-year-old Tair, Liron (30) and Tagel (26) – were raised in this region to parents with Yemenite heritage and with three other siblings, surrounded by camels, chickens and goats. 'It was like growing up in Little House On the Prairie,' Tair describes. 'Being in such a beautiful place that's very open and isolated meant we could imagine and create things out of nothing.'

The trio's creation came musically as A-Wa (pronounced ay-wah), meaning 'yeah' in Arabic slang – because 'it's short, it's positive and it's catchy' – and while it may sound modern, the music's roots are grounded in traditional Yemenite folk. These ancient songs about love and protest were written and sung by women in a Yemeni-Arabic dialect and have been passed down through generations. A-Wa's debut album *Habib Galbi* (*The One I Love*), which came out in November, comprises 12 of these tunes recorded for a new audience. 'We thought it would be amazing for our first album to go with the source,' explains Tair, 'with music from our family roots combined with new styles that we love, such as hip hop and reggae.'

Other influences, Tair elaborates, include Bob Marley, Motown, prog-rock from the 70s and great singers such as Ella Fitzgerald, Aretha Franklin and Michael Jackson. 'Music to us is like a treasure, so we're always trying to find new inspirations, but the visual that accompanies our music is also very important to us.' Tair is referring to the way the sisters dress, which follows their music in combining the new with the old. 'We love Yemenite embroidery and jewellery, as well as hip-hop street fashion. We also really love the Moroccan photographer Hassan Hajjaj.'

Dubbed the 'Andy Warhol of Marrakech', Hajjaj is heavily inspired by pop art and it's clear to see his effect on the Haim women. Their outfits pop with colours and patterns, especially evidenced in the video for their debut single. Also titled 'Habib Galbi', the band can be seen in it striding through the desert in hot pink jellabiyas – something that has helped towards their popularity amongst Muslim audiences. 'We heard that in Yemen little girls are inspired by our video,' Tair enthuses. 'They feel like we do something to empower them as women, that we say and act like they want to, but can't. And of course they love the groove and the new approach that we give the songs.'

Views of the 'Habib Galbi' video are racing towards the two million mark and the single has become the first-ever Arabic language song to top the Israeli charts. Could the trio be a sign of the shifting cultural tides to Israel's acceptance of its Mizrahi communities? The Mizrahi – Jews from Arab lands – have traditionally faced discrimination in Israel and their communities are some of the poorest in the country. But Tair explains that this wasn't their experience growing up in Shaharut. 'I think when our grandparents came to Israel it was hard for them,' she reflects, 'because they had to speak Hebrew and almost forget the Yemenite dialect. But our mum's family is from Europe, with Moroccan roots, so we're a mix of cultures and we just didn't feel like that was a strange thing, because Israel is a country of immigrants.'

Today the sisters live in Tel Aviv, when they're not touring the surrounding continents that is, but they might not have reached their current status were it not for one key name: Tomer Yosef. Known for being the frontman of Israeli-American fusion outfit Balkan Beat Box, Yosef discovered one of A-Wa's homemade videos on YouTube and saw the potential. Utilising his own Eastern European-meets-reggae influences, Yosef produced A-Wa's debut album and injected new life into their music, which was originally more conventional, as Tair divulges. 'We did start with a more traditional sound, but our plan was always to take it to modern production and combine it with electronic beats because we don't think it's interesting to bring forward the tradition as is, but to give it our own twist. That's the beauty of it: to give something new to people's ears.'

The band's approach blends electronic dance music and hip-hop rhythms with melodious Arabic chanting that A-Wa associate with their grandfather on their father's side, who emigrated from Yemen to Israel in 1949. 'Grandpa knew the Torah by heart,' Tair tells us, 'and he used to pray beautifully with Yemenite pronunciation; it sounded like he was singing. And at family weddings and celebrations there would be Yemenite cuisine and music, so we fell in love with these traditions as kids.' It's no wonder that A-Wa maintain so many of them, at one concert they even sold jachnun, a slow-baked Yemenite-Jewish/Israeli puff pastry 'to give the audience a big Yemenite celebration'.

At the moment A-Wa continue to tour *Habib Galbi* with their four-strong band of musicians, but Tair reveals that they've already begun work on their second record and have many plans for the coming year. 'We really want to release more cool videos – very artistic and inspiring – and we'd love to collaborate with great musicians and artists from all over the world, from art to fashion, to continue performing live, and to grow as women as well as artists and continue spreading love and music in this world.' It just goes to show that even from small beginnings can come big achievements.

AFTERWORD

DAVID DANGOOR CBE DL

My family's association with *Jewish Renaissance* magazine began with my father, the Iraqi philanthropist Sir Naim Dangoor. In 1964, with the political situation and anti-Semitism in Iraq worsening, my father left his home in Baghdad and settled in London to begin a new life, almost from scratch. He soon became a successful businessman but increasingly felt he wanted to create something for the international Iraqi diaspora.

In 1971, he founded *The Scribe* magazine, featuring articles about Iraqi life and culture. Thirty years later, after an interview with Janet Levin for her new magazine *Jewish Renaissance,* my father offered to support the launch of the magazine and suggested devoting a section of it to the history and traditions of Iraqi Jews. He contributed articles and photos for the section and in her interview with him, Janet noted, 'A conversation with Naim Dangoor is full of surprises. He is a man who does not mind sticking his neck out.'

JR's special report on the Jews of Iraq, in its first issue in October 2001, was such a hit that it gave birth to the popular 'Passport' series, which continues to focus on Jewish communities around the world. In 2011, when the magazine celebrated its tenth year, my father sponsored a bumper issue featuring picks of the previous decade, including interviews with the director Mike Leigh, the writer David Grossman and the former Chief Rabbi Lord Jonathan Sacks.

My father's support continued over the years and in July 2016, I had the honour of continuing that involvement and becoming the magazine's honorary president. The July 2016 issue also marked the launch of 'Sephardi Renaissance', a special section focusing on the culture and history of Sephardi and Mizrahi

Jewish communities in the UK and beyond. These were communities that, as I put it at the time, 'had something of a low profile in UK Jewish life'.

Kicking off that first Sephardi section were articles including a piece on Baghdad's Farhud (*pogrom*); a report on a former bus drivers' café in Essex that had been turned into a Sephardi synagogue; and a piece on Sephardi wedding henna parties. Later issues have featured interviews with the Sephardi and Mizrahi musicians such as Yair Dalal, A-Wa and Liraz; a report on the archaeologists conserving Jewish sites in war torn Syria and an exploration of the lives of eighteenth-century Sephardi women. *JR* was one of the first UK Jewish publications to fully embrace the diversity of the Jewish world.

I have been delighted to have also been involved in many *JR* initiatives over the years, including events at Jewish Book Week, the UK Jewish Film Festival, establishing the first young Jewish Journalist prize and, of course, in supporting this very special book. It has been a pleasure to have watched *JR* grow in its professionalism and confidence – all while maintaining its commitment to engaging content, beautiful design and a joyful embrace of global Jewish culture. There is surely nothing else like it in the UK today and I am certain my father, Naim, would be proud that it has come this far. Happy Birthday, *JR*!

AUTHOR BIOGRAPHIES

NATHAN ABRAMS

Nathan Abrams is Professor of Film at Bangor University and director of the Centre for Film, Television and Screen Studies. He lectures, writes and broadcasts widely on film and co-founded the journal *Jewish Film and New Media*. Nathan's books include *The Bloomsbury Companion to Stanley Kubrick* (with IQ Hunter, 2021), *Eyes Wide Shut: Stanley Kubrick and the Making of His Final Film* (with Robert Kolker, 2019), *Stanley Kubrick: New York Jewish Intellectual* (2018), *Hidden in Plain Sight: Jews and Jewishness in British Film, Television, and Popular Culture* (2016), and *The New Jew in Film: Exploring Jewishness and Judaism in Contemporary Cinema* (2012).

DAVID BENMAYER

David Benmayer is a trustee of *JR* and a former chief executive of Renaissance Publishing, having succeeded Janet Levin in the role. He studied history at the London School of Economics, where he received his undergraduate and masters degrees, focusing on the British Empire in the late Victorian and Edwardian eras, as well as the Jewish experience during this period. He can still be found writing on these topics in the pages of *JR*. Prior to his involvement with *JR*, David was a public sector strategy consultant. He now works in his family's textile business, situated in the heart of London's East End.

MONICA BOHM-DUCHEN

Monica Bohm-Duchen is an independent writer, lecturer and curator. Based in London, the institutes she has worked for include Birkbeck, University of London, the Courtauld Institute of Art, Sotheby's Institute of Art, Tate, the National Gallery and the Royal Academy of Arts. Her publications include *After Auschwitz: Responses to the Holocaust in Contemporary Art* (1995), *Rubies and Rebels: Jewish Female Identity in Contemporary British Art* (1996) and *Art and the Second World War* (2014). She is the initiator and Creative Director of Insiders/Outsiders, an ongoing arts festival celebrating the contribution of refugees from Nazi Europe to British culture and is on the editorial board of *Jewish Renaissance*.

BRYAN CHEYETTE

Bryan Cheyette is Professor of Modern Literature at the University of Reading. His early publications were influential accounts of literary anti-semitism and include *Constructions of 'the Jew' in English Literature and Society: Racial Representations 1875–1945* (1995). He has also published extensively on British-Jewish literature, including an anthology, *Contemporary Jewish Writing in Britain and Ireland* (1998). His recent work includes *Diasporas of the Mind: Jewish/Postcolonial Writing and the Nightmare of History* (2014) and *Ghetto: A Very Short Introduction* (2020).

JUDI HERMAN

Judi Herman is a freelance writer and broadcaster. She is *JR*'s arts and podcast editor, as well as a regular contributor of reviews and features to *JR*'s magazine and blog. Judi also freelances for the BBC and whatsonstage.com. She has an MA in Performing Arts from Middlesex University, and has written several stage-shows, including *How the West End Was Won*, celebrating Jewish life in London's West End, and *Stones of Kolin*, a musical play charting 600 years of Jewish life in a small Czech town, performed in London and the Czech Republic. Judi also has a background in public relations, including PR for theatre.

VANESSA PALOMA-ELBAZ

Vanessa Paloma Elbaz is a research associate at the Faculty of Music of the University of Cambridge and Peterhouse. She received her PhD from the Research Center for Middle Eastern and Mediterranean Studies of Sorbonne Paris Cité University, with *félicitations du jury*. Her research has been funded by the Fulbright, Marie Curie Horizon 2020 Actions, the Posen Foundation and American Institute for Maghrib Studies, among others. She has written for Cambridge University Press, Oxford University Press, *Tablet*, *The Forward* and numerous academic and mainstream journals. She founded KHOYA: Jewish Morocco Sound Archive in 2012 in Casablanca.

REBECCA TAYLOR

Rebecca Taylor is the editor of *JR*. She studied English at Cambridge University and then spent nine years living in Tokyo, where she worked at *The Japan Times* newspaper. After returning to London, she worked at the *Guardian* for several years and was the news editor at *Time Out London* for ten years before joining *JR* in 2015. Her work has appeared in several anthologies, and she has interviewed everyone from Tony Blair and Boris Johnson to Zadie Smith and Jerry Springer.

The History Press

The destination for history
www.thehistorypress.co.uk